Praise for *The Magick of Bending Time in Your Sacred Business*

With this delightful book, Britt Bolnick offers us magickal and busy women a surprising, compassionate and effective path to taking charge of our time in a way that feels AMAZING and not dreadful and oppressive like all those "bro" takes on the subject.

–Carolyn Elliot, Author of **Existential Kink** and founder of WEALTH: the alchemical community where leaders come into their full power.

"This powerful how-to guide is brimming with straightforward strategies to overcome the key fears associated with managing and effectively using your time to get your brilliance out into the world.

"I highly recommend using this book – and Britt's wisdom – to learn how to make your time work for you without sacrificing your sanity or freedom."

- **Barbara Huson**, author of **Rewire for Wealth** and **Sacred Success.**

"This book, like Britt herself, is a treasure trove of valuable, real life tips on how to marry your business with your LIFE. She combines practicality with magic and harsh reality with dreams. I gained so much power from Britt's wisdom and lost (thank God) so much anxiety. She helped me steer my business boat to smooth sailing because she helped me find my 'why,' my center and my sanity. This book. Yes. Read it."

—**Leigh Kellis**, Founder, The Holy Donut

"This isn't REALLY a book... it's a manifesto, a call to arms, a spiritual take on what we traditionally know as "time blocking" that every witchy woman NEEDS in order to be in complete control of her greatest asset... her time (and energy).

It's rare to come across the perfect collaboration of practical and spiritual in a 'business book,' but Britt's take on Sacred Structure, and why we need it, is exactly that.

Britt actually manages to make time management sexy... weird, I know! But it's true. My entire CONTEXT on time management has been forever shifted.

If you're ready to ditch the 'cult of busy,' take your power back, and have access to a tool that provides both day-to-day structure as well as complete freedom, flexibility, and choice... then you need this (not) book."

—**Jen Spivak**, Founder, The Ad Girls

"It's no surprise that Britt Bolnick literally wrote the book on bending time! Britt cuts right to the chase and wastes no time in sharing her magic, wisdom, and insight into how to live a powerful life and create space for the things that light you up.

Anyone who has thought, 'I just don't have time to do…xyz,' needs to read this book to see that the possibilities are endless."

—**Sarah Evelyn Spiegel,** Founder, Samudra Studio

"Please don't pick up this book and expect it will solve your time management issues. That would be like buying household cleaning products in the hopes that they will clean your house.

The Magick of Bending Time will have you do the work. And this work WORKS.

Britt will guide, coach and whisper insights for your soul to awaken. If you want something to fix you, duct tape is in aisle 3. This book will heal you because there is nothing broken. You will see what is available for capture by fearlessly easing into a sacred practice that becomes routine for you and you alone. This is not a one-time event; this is a practice to come back to and keep alive.

Here's the catch, if you are a business owner, a corporate desk jockey, or run a kick-ass household with dreams of something more… you WILL get value out of the practices. If you are Magical with a capital Witch or just someone (like me) that wishes to be more magical and less muggle, this book speaks to all of us. No prior experience with anything other than a time management catastrophe and desire to NOT be forced into a pretty box.

This book is for the magical muggles in us all. We can bend time. We can delight and engage in our lives authentically. And collectively, we can acknowledge the hustle and boss bitch in all of us, and let her put her feet up, because the witch is in charge."

—**Kim Crean**, Leadership Keynote speaker and humorist

"I was in my mid-twenties when I hauled my butt to a big auditorium in Boston to attend my first time management seminar. All excited with the results they promised, I forked over what felt like a MASSIVE chunk of change for their fancy schmancy calendar system. I hoped my investment would finally help the creative, magical empathic young woman I was, to be more productive and organized. Like Britt Bolnick, I perceived myself as lousy with time management. I won't even begin to go into my challenges with punctuality!

Even with all its bells and whistles, as you might imagine, that popular calendar system didn't cut it for me. Try as I might, I couldn't consistently create daily to-do lists and rank them based on priority. In the same way that I inevitably lost steam for any rigid diet and exercise regimen, this approach to time management only worked for a few weeks at best.

It wasn't until Britt led me through her Sacred Structure that I found something that worked for me. This is because instead of allocating every spare moment of my weeks, days, hours and minutes to achieve some task or goal, Britt invited me to claim what mattered to me. Britt helped me to focus on my desires first and to identify the things that sucked the life and enthusiasm out of my days. It started by saying yes to what I actually wanted and to gradually drop or delegate the rest. This process helped me to pivot from a thriving brick and mortar business to an even more aligned virtual one. Today I have even more control over my time than I did with my previous dollars for hours business that loaded my appointment book but left me no wiggle room to adjust for life's inevitable unpredictabilities. The system outlined in this book has allowed me to carve out the time and space to write and launch my own first book AND to be a collaborating author for another. My life is far sweeter, quieter and ease-full than it was a decade ago. I know that Britt's Sacred Structure is one of the magic ingredients that made it possible.

The Magick of Bending Time in Your Sacred Business takes all of Britt's brilliance and know-how and distills it down to a doable system that works. Even though I started working with this system many years ago, I have found the questions and suggestions both validating and refreshing. Time really is one of our most sacred and precious commodities. Sadly I see way too many of us go from work crisis, to dirty dish, to dirty diaper, to family emergency, to crashing on the couch binge-watching some random series only to wonder where the day went as our exhausted head hits the pillow at the end of it.

On one hand this book is about time. On the other it's about SO MUCH MORE. This is a book that shows you how to identify where you're hemorrhaging energy and how to turn it around. It's a book that encourages you to say YES to self-care, to say YES to your passion, to say YES to support. This is a book that shows you how to put your own oxygen mask on first. This book is for anyone who knows that life can be more than trudging from one responsibility to the next. This book is for people who feel sick and tired of spinning their wheels and are ready to make a difference in this world. This book is the antidote to the fear that more success equals more sacrifice. This book leads you to answers contained in your own sacred heart. This book is magic."

—**Jennifer Elizabeth Moore**, Author of **Empathic Mastery**, Mentor & Master Trainer for EFT International

"As a biz owner, it is CRUCIAL I stay focused on how I use my time. When I'm in the day-to day depths of my biz it's easy to lose sight of why time management is so vital and give into my habit of slamming my schedule full as a form of self sabotage and people-pleasing.

Britt's book is SO magically helpful in that she helps me remember I'm not alone on this journey, gives guidance on how to lovingly identify and release how my fear of success and scarcity mindset shows up with my time management, provides exercises that helped me figure out MY aligned schedule, and action steps to make that dream calendar my reality.

After reading this book I'm in love with my calendar and how it supports me in living my best life.

—**Lisa Presley,** The Productivity Pixie

"The Magick of Bending Time in Your Sacred Business: Time management for freedom-seeking, entrepreneurial women and organizational skeptics by Britt Bolnick is an incredibly empowering book.

Written with energy and humor, it is the perfect mix of real-life insights, thoughtful questions and proven, actionable tools that can be applied to every aspect of your life to create sustainable, long-lasting change."

—**Amanda Lopes**, The Virtual Assistant's Confidence Coach, Business Consultant & Systems Expert

"Britt Bolnick is a master at teaching you how to create more time and space for all the things you want. This book contains a treasure trove of easy yet powerful tools that are like a magic wand for your schedule, your boundaries, and ultimately, your well-being."

—**Joanna Lindenbaum**, Founder of the Applied Depth Practitioner Institute

The Magick of Bending Time speaks to the practical magic we can all use in REAL TIME to create an opening, a portal, that helps us to liberate ourselves from the old stories that bind us and slow us down, so we can make the leap into the life we really want to be living.

Britt's book is not only an awakening to what's possible for us as women leaders, it's a practical how-to manual that will show you exactly how to break free and go to the next level.

Beyond the practical and deep value of this book, Britt's heart and soul is invested in seeing women thrive. She is a deeply appreciated leader in our community."

—**Kaeleya Rayne**, Founder and CEO of the Unstoppable Feminine Leaders Movement

"'**The Magick Of Bending Time in Your Sacred Business**' by Britt Bolnick is a deeply thought-provoking conversation with our inner skeptic + Spiritual-BossWitch.

Britt Bolnick serves up platefuls of deeply intuitive "real talk" to the serial entrepreneur + inner biz-witch's soul. This highly consumable binge read is brimming with sacred feminine empowerment, and Britt's laser-targeted time management advice is magickal gold! She shows you how to target deep fear-based beliefs subconsciously holding women down, and helps plant healthier mantras as tools for time management and financial growth.

Her approach is a constructive and tangible strategy that nurtures a positive + successful mindset approach. She delves deep into her pool of experience as a strong business woman and coach to deliver premium value to the women she attracts in this fulfilling read!

Britt's 'Sacred Structure' method works by delving deep into the entrepreneurial woman's psyche, and gently guides her to methodically root-out those negative + outdated businesses models, implanted skeptical self-imagery, and the number one toxicity to sacred feminine empowerment - The Patriarchal Kryptonite - toxic masculinity and language etched on our inner temple walls.

Britt Bolnick masterfully luminates the path forward for the next millennia of highly motivated business women, establishes a truly powerful + magickal brand of New Age BizCraft, and guides the reader on a magickal journey to time and money freedom."

—**Beth Matthews**, Online Marketing & Business Strategist| Funnel Educator | Online Solopreneur

We're in a powerful time of reclaiming the feminine, both on a systemic level, as well as in business. Britt's wisdom on how to create more time helps readers glean tools to create space for their most beloved projects, and for their hopes, dreams and visions to come to fruition NOW – not years from now or sometime down the road. This is a call for women to remember their innate magical power, to create businesses that inspire freedom and flow, and lead their heart-centered missions from the feminine.

—**Ashley Burnett**, Writer and Women's Business and Leadership Coach

THE
MAGICK
OF
Bending Time
IN YOUR
SACRED BUSINESS

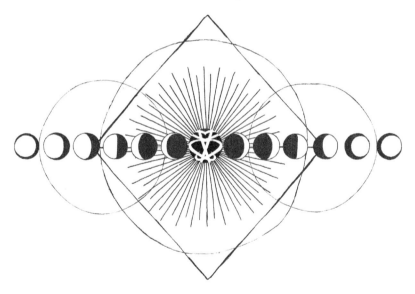

Time Management for Freedom-Seeking
Entrepreneurial Women and Organizational Skeptics

BRITT BOLNICK

ISBN: 978-1-7368272-0-8

Library of Congress Control Number: 2021904721

Printed in Portland, Maine by Britt Bolnick

Book cover and interior graphics by Christi Cooper, Cooper & Heart Creative

The publisher has strived to be as accurate and complete as possible in the creation of this book. The views expressed in this work are solely those of the author.

The advice and strategies found within may not be suitable for every situation. This work is sold with the understanding that neither the author nor the publisher is held responsible for the results accrued from the advice in this book. Use of this book does not establish any type of advisory, coaching, or professional relationship with the author or publisher.

While all attempts have been made to verify information provided for this publication, the publisher assumes no responsibility for errors, omissions, or contrary interpretation of the subject matter herein.

For more information, visit www.InArmsCoaching.com.

For bulk book orders, contact Britt directly at Britt@InArmsCoaching.com.

Dedication

For Bella Nysa, my best person. Your birth led me to this path. Being your Mama is the best gift I'll ever get.

Table of Contents

Chapter 1

Why WE Need YOU
To Have Time Freedom

Time is the most precious commodity in life.

How you spend your time is what differentiates a life that is simply tolerable from a life that's deeply satisfying, full of all the things you love.

How you're spending your hours is how you're spending your days.

And how you're spending your days is how you're spending your life.

We either live our lives the way we dream of, or we dream of someday living our lives.

If that sounds scary or familiar, YOU ARE IN THE RIGHT PLACE.

I'm about to blow the lid off of how you've been using your time.

(In the best way possible.)

I'm about to show you some serious, (yet easy), life-altering magick in the realm of managing your time.

It's time to stop giving your life away, one hour at a time.

For you, your family and friends and, frankly, in support of the impact you want to have with your work.

If you're reading this book, you have a gift to offer the world.

And no matter what your contribution is, it matters. We need you doing work you LOVE, that contributes to the change you want to see in the world.

The only way for you to be able to be fully and completely present in (and enjoying) your life is if you are the keeper (and bender) of your time. Feeling sovereign over your time is one of the deepest feelings of freedom you can experience. And yet SO FEW people reach that point of empowerment–when your time is spent doing 95% ONLY what you LOVE.

We are living in an incredibly powerful period in our collective evolution...

Any moment in history where there is massive unrest, injustice, fear, lack and disparity **is a moment in time that is begging us to rebel against the powers that be to create something new.**

As the mothers among us know...birth is messy. It's painful. It can feel like dying. You might want to be ANYWHERE BUT IN THAT MOMENT.

And then...there's a WHOOSH...and there's new life. And rest. And peace. And joy.

We're pushing hard right now, and shit is JAMMED in that birth canal.

{AND I'M WRITING THIS BEFORE THE 2020 PRESIDENTIAL ELECTION, Goddess help us.}

This moment in the United States, at least, is a moment when there is such a heightened sense of injustice, of fear, of hatred, of division that for some of us it feels almost intolerable.

There is work to be done.

We need all hands on deck to collectively push us out into the next phase...and I'm fighting for us to come out into the light of what exists beyond this painful and frightening time.

I believe we are on the verge of reimagining the necessary and incredible possibilities life holds.

And you, wise, heart-centered woman, have hands that can help carry us further.

If you've been called to pick this book up then I'm certain that you have a mission, work, a calling, that is absolutely non-negotiable for you to get out into the world.

You might have a gift, a tool, a process, maybe even products or live offerings, that lead people towards making some sort of a shift in their lives. You have work that matters: that supports a cause, that feeds something meaningful and desirable in your life, that feeds your family (or needs to), that contributes to the change that you want to see for the world.

And you're a powerful, driven, magickal woman deeply in service to your vision.

Here's the issue.

It has historically been difficult (if not impossible) for you to get out of your own way.

There's an AWFUL lot to do in your life. Your plate is SO full, at all times.

You might have kids, elderly parents, animals, paycheck jobs, passion projects, friends, relatives, self-care, a relationship to tend to – most likely a combo of the above.

You're trying to get your work out into the world while ALSO attempting to balance:

→ Eating better/cooking healthy food

→ Moving your body; getting outdoors

→ Raising a baby, child(ren), or caring for an elderly relative

→ Keeping your house from looking condemned

→ Juggling a bridge job – work that's not your calling but pays the bills until your calling DOES

→ Volunteering for causes that matter deeply to you

→ Sleeping (please don't skip this one)

→ Praying, meditating, practicing magick, being part of a spiritual community

{What else would you add to this list?}

And if you're also trying to grow your magickal work, get seen, become known, grow your clients, impact, and **INCOME...**

Those 24 hours a day go like water through your fingers. I want to help you stop the leakage of your time so that you can USE it for your highest purposes and set it up according to what you love MOST.

I want you to feel like you have the time you want for yourself, your work, your vision, and all the things that nurture you in your life.

So let's jump in!

Finding the leaks

First things first, you need to identify the hole in the bucket.

Not all things that take your time, energy and focus are created equal. On the next page is a short meditation to feel into how you're expending your energy now. DON'T SKIP IT.

Tool: Find Where Your Energy Is Leaking

Note: If you'd rather close your eyes and hear me lead you through this meditation, just go to the bonus page I've built for you with resources that I want you to have: https://InArmsCoaching.com/bookfreegift

Get in a comfortable place and close your eyes.
Put one hand over your heart (against your skin) and one on your belly, and take three deep breaths, letting your belly expand into your hands as you do so.

Begin to imagine yourself in a circle, and around you are all the people and situations that you're giving energy to.

See each person/situation clearly as you look around the circle, and note an energetic cord connecting you to each person/situation – some are thick because there's a lot of energy that you're giving, and some are thinner.

Note which cords are thickest and how that feels to you – is the energy you're giving in this instance being returned?

Note if the energy you're giving feels voluntary, pleasurable, and consensual.

Which cords connect you to people/situations where you're getting less than you give, or it's not something

you WANT to be giving energy to?
Which connections feel even somewhat non-consensual,
or unpleasant, or just DRAINING?

Now, take a second to go around the circle and UNPLUG
yourself from each and every person or situation.

Take the unplugged end and PLUG IT INTO YOURSELF
for a minute. And feel into the sensation of all your
energy feeding YOU, directly. Imagine your feet on the
ground, the energy that's available to you right now if you
were wholly feeding yourself and no one else. Take a few
deep breaths here.

And now, in your mind's eye, open your eyes and look
back around that circle.

Whom and what do you consciously WANT to be giving
energy to? Plug yourself back into them with full consent
and intention.
And see how that feels.

Take three deep breaths, and begin to return to the room
you're sitting in. Open your eyes and grab a pen and paper.

Write down two lists: the people and situations you're
giving energy to that you enjoy, and the people and situations that you're giving energy to that you DON'T enjoy.

Unplugging yourself in your mind isn't an immediate,
permanent solution.

It's going to take a little more work than that to perma-
nently sever draining expenses of energy in your life,

but seeing WHAT'S draining you and even unplugging yourself for a few minutes at a time WILL begin to have an effect on you. And it's important to see clearly what's draining, and what's feeding you right back.

There are a few reasons I'm upset enough to write a book to teach you how to magickally bend time to do your bidding.

1. RIGHT NOW we need all hands – YOUR hands – on deck. We need our healers, magicians, luminaries, leaders, creatives, visionaries, light-workers...now, possibly more than ever.

    We need you rested, focused, supported, and powerful as all fuck. Right here. Right now.

    And if you're magickal as all hell, but EXHAUSTED, distracted, disempowered, frustrated, overwhelmed, unsupported...then you're not going to be able to effectively focus on that thing or those things that you do so expertly.

2. The second reason I'm upset and writing this book that you hold in your hands is that I know, from over 15 years of coaching women, that **we often have a fear of what "success" will cost us.** *We keep ourselves small so we don't have to make sacrifices or*

compromises that feel uncomfortable, unwanted, or sacrificial. And this fear can become the death of your vision, even of your actual business.

For instance, many of my clients are afraid that if their business takes off, it will COST them time: to sleep; put the kids to bed; have a relaxed family dinner every night; practice self-care; have regular, unscheduled time.

This creates a fear that lurks beneath the surface. You might not be aware of it in your day-to-day life.

You might think, "But, of COURSE I want to be successful! Of COURSE I want to use my time like a MoFo bad-ass to create MORE money, more clients, more visibility. DUH."

BUT: there's a fear in the back of your mind that if you DO create that thing you want, you'll lose your free time. You'll have to hire support, and that's uncomfortable for a variety of reasons. You'll have to put in more hours, work, and nights while sleeping less and being less available to the people you love.

And even though IT'S NOT TRUE...this fear can cause you to sabotage your own success.

Because if you believe that's the case, it doesn't matter what you think on the surface. Your subconscious is jamming its foot down on the brakes like you're about to go careening over a cliff to certain death. And there you are, foot on the gas, all like, "WHY WON'T THIS BITCH MOVE?"

Insight Exercise

In what ways do YOU believe that success will cost you?

★ _____

★ _____

★ _____

★ _____

★ _____

We grow up in a culture where the business model given to us is that of the *patriarchal model of leadership*: this is where you hear things like, "No pain, no gain." "Hustle." "Boss Mode." "CEO mindset."

In the professional world there's a common belief that if you're not KILLING yourself, if you're not working your fingers to the bone, if you're not SACRIFICING...*then you're not worthy of success.*

There's a belief that you have to CHOOSE: be a good mom or be a successful entrepreneur or businesswoman.

Many women feel pulled between being present at home or being present at the office or the laptop. It feels like there's never enough TIME.

Many of my clients struggle with guilt. When you're working you're feeling guilty that you're not doing more of the things you love. And then the guilt returns again when you do the things you love because now you're not working. It feels like you can't win. (*Don't worry, keep reading, we 're going to get to the part where it doesn't have to be like this.*)

The result is long days of multi-tasking, extended work days that spill into the evening, coupled with GUILT and overwhelm.

Here's the thing though: while this is a deeply undesirable state for us to feel stuck in, it's not bad for EVERYONE. Someone profits from you feeling this way.

For instance, the powers-that-be, the rulers of the toxic patriarchy, the people who profit from capitalism and those in the corporate world WANT you scattered, overwhelmed, pulled between things you love and exhausted...they all PROFIT from you feeling that way.

Why?

Because feeling that way makes us all more reactionary, more depleted, less focused, and deeply disempowered. **THAT makes us more manipulatable, more likely to follow, more likely to obey and toe the line.** Feeling this way contributes to the consumer culture and we're more likely to buy shit we don't need, develop addiction issues, rely on crappy food, and watch more TV when we're feeling disconnected and on the hamster wheel of depletion.

Most of you who are building a business, getting the work you love out into the world, struggling to make time for everything you love, and trying to BALANCE it all have (until now) **only had the status quo to follow.**

And it's not working. For any of us. *Because most of us want something different than the cultural definition of success, with all its hurry, fluster, and emphasis on material status symbols.*

This patriarchal structure comes from the male-centered 1950s model of building a business where you got to check out of all the real details of life so you can spend all day pursuing your dreams and ambitions (*and you're a man in this example, BTW, cuz there weren't really any women playing this game back then, and even if they were, they had to act like men*).

That's why you had a WIFEY at home taking care of EVERY other aspect of your life: kids, pets, home, food, family, cleaning, social calendar, etc.

Don't know 'bout you, but I don't currently have a wifey.

In fact, I AM the WIFEY.

And even if I HAD a wifey, she wouldn't be a house-wifey, which is what's REQUIRED to uphold the patriarchal model of building a business that most of us have had.

SO.

Many women like you who are healers, visionaries, lightworkers, magick makers, leaders...are afraid of unleashing your full power and potential because you KNOW you've only got 24-in-7 <u>and they already go so fast</u> and maybe you ALREADY feel like you're dropping balls...

SO HOW THE HELL do you make MORE time to nurture your calling, business, and work? I mean, we all get the SAME 24/7, right?

Bottom line: that's why many women like you stay small (mostly unconsciously), because of what you're unknowingly afraid it will cost you. That makes me CRAZY because I know we NEED you. I want you out in the world doing your thing and KILLING it.

I want you to be doing work that sets your soul on fire, FILLS your bank account, and enables you to get your damn oxygen mask on so that you can battle the way ONLY you are called to.

{BY THE WAY...

You don't have to be a metaphorical sword-swinger for this to apply to you. Your work COULD be giving delicious, healing massages AND being present for yourself and your family.

It could be running the family business with all your heart and attention, and then STILL being able to be present, focused and happy for family time or YOU-time.

It could be making jewelry that makes people feel special when they put it on AND being fully present for board games at night or yoga in the morning.}

Is this POSSIBLE? Who the HELL is THIS woman, talking this crazy-talk? (We'll get to that in a bit. For now just try to suspend your disbelief long enough to get the gift this book can offer you: YOUR TIME BACK.)

I'm so psyched that you've picked up this book on creating a way to exist with time that works FOR you.

The content and exercises I'm going to teach you in the following pages have completely transformed my clients' lives and schedules, and I know it can do the same for you.

When I started this journey I was a newly-single, solo mama of a toddler.

I married a man who basically gave me the best thing in my whole life (my Kid) and then left us for a 23-year-old dog walker.

I had sunk every penny I had (including money from a lawsuit settlement) into a two-family home in Brooklyn, New York City, for my new family. Because what's a WISER thing to do with a bunch of cash than to buy NYC real estate, right? *How could THAT go wrong?* I laugh now (you'll see why) but at the time it seemed the smartest, most secure thing I could do with some cash and a new baby.

When the Kid's dad left less than a year later, leaving me with the Kid (thank Goddess), a 6-7 nights-a-week waitressing and bartending job in Manhattan (an hour away) and a mortgage I couldn't pay (oh, and no consistent child support), I broke.

Physically and emotionally devastated with no one to watch the Kid at night and no money to pay the mortgage, I moved back in with my mother, who lived across the street from the restaurant where I worked. She could thankfully stay with little Boo while I worked every shift I could.

I lost the building and with it, every penny I had sunk into it.

The Kid and I spent the next three years living together in the bedroom where I grew up.

There were silver linings, though.

Baby Daddy signed away sole custody to me and disappeared on and off for five years, before disappearing for good when she was 7.

This meant I had the sheer luxury of not having to base the next seventeen years on shared custody with an asshole, which would have chained me to NYC.

I also didn't get child support from him on a regular basis, then got none at all, but I felt that allowing him to walk away and not cause trouble could possibly be worth it. *I was REALLY right about that – current Me gives Past Me a HUGE hug for trusting her gut on that one.* I just planned to figure out a way to support my own damned, amazing Kid.

Over the next year as I started to heal, caught up on badly needed rest, and got my head clear, *I realized that we actually had unlimited possibility in front of us.* **We could do anything.**

We could go anywhere. We didn't have to stay in New York City. We could create our future based on what worked best for JUST the two of us. I knew it was important to focus my energy at that point and be conscious and intentional about what I wanted to create for us.

So I wrote down what I knew I wanted for our life. (I LOVE a good list. So head-clearing.)

1. **I wanted to be able to raise the Kid by myself** without depending on childcare. Ideally, I wanted to homeschool and make our own schedule, which meant being able to create work that could happen around our schedule, not the other way around.

2. **I wanted, with all my heart, to leave New York City.** We had been to visit friends in Maine recently and more than anything I wanted to move there. I knew that was a few years away but it helped me to conceptualize work that gave me geographical flexibility so I could pick up and move to another state without losing work.

3. **I wanted to do something I cared DEEPLY about.** I wanted everything in my life to be passion-based and fulfilling. Not that I didn't love my restaurant job (I actually did really enjoy it most of the time) but it wasn't fulfilling my soul. I knew I wanted to support other women, especially as I emerged from the darkest years of my life. I wanted to feel like I was extending a hand back to other women in some way.

Insight Exercise

What do YOU want for yourself?

Make a list now of the things you know you want.

This list is not exhaustive, but it's important to start somewhere. Getting these things down on paper is one of the first steps in directing your time and energy towards where you want to go!

★ _____

★ _____

★ _____

★ _____

★ _____

With the clarity from my list I hired a business coach to hold my hand and guide me. It cost me an extra few shifts a month to be able to pay her, but I knew I couldn't do this by myself and that I needed structure, support, guidance, and mentorship.

I also knew that I had VERY little time per week to start and grow this business and I couldn't afford to waste time throwing spaghetti at the wall and seeing what stuck.

Although I knew a LOT about coaching and supporting women, I didn't know anything about starting OR running a business. I needed help understanding things like marketing and promoting myself, growing a community, setting up my website and newsletter, and structuring my offerings so the ideal women could find me and benefit from my support.

This piece was really important. I was building a business that asked other women to trust me to get support with their needs, to understand they couldn't do it alone or by themselves, and to take the leap of faith to invest in themselves.

If I weren't doing all the above, myself, I would feel out of integrity. I have always made sure I'm walking my talk and allowing myself the support I have built a business out of encouraging other women to invest in.

Thus, In Arms Coaching (IAC) was born. At that time I had about 3 to 4 hours a week to focus on EVERYTHING I needed to do to start and then GROW the work that I was depending on to eventually fully support myself, the Kid, and the dog. (That was the amount of time I had child-free, that I wasn't already working.) I was exhausted ALL the time.

If I were a car at that point I would have been doing that sputtering, stop-and-go jerking that precedes getting stranded on the side of the road because the gas tank is EMPTY. One of the reasons why support was so crucial to me at that point was because I literally felt that I was at a "do or die" place where if I didn't make SURE I was doing something different, I wouldn't be able to get up in the morning in the very near future.

I had to do something differently to get different results.

In the early days of IAC I was offering parenting coaching based on the work I did in prisons with incarcerated moms and their infants (SUPER cool program that combined parenting education with literacy skills). I had my Master of Education degree and I had done a LOT of inner work and educating myself in getting ready to be the Kid's parent and raise her as a happy, healthy child. I had also worked really hard to look at what worked for me about the way my parents raised me, and what DIDN'T, so I didn't blindly repeat parenting methods that I didn't enjoy myself as a kid.

I also had a "deep why" around natural and attachment parenting – the idea that our babies are sensitive, empathic beings whom we get to build a relationship with based on unconditional love and respect. I was passionate about women being supported in conscious parenting from a place of healing our OWN wounds, not passing them on to our children, and supporting our babies in growing up to be loving, empathic, considerate and confident adults.

However, I noticed that the women who were coming to me also wanted more general life-coaching on reconnecting with and making time for themselves, focusing on their partnerships, growing their self-esteem, and building a life they loved. So IAC morphed away from parenting coaching to more general life-coaching for busy moms. I had clients very soon after "opening" my doors.

Here was the issue, though: I had a LOT on my plate, and very little time in which to do it.

And the story I told myself was that I was disorganized, terrible with time management, and couldn't stick to plans.

Because that's something we do, as women. We take an unfair situation and blame our inability to succeed within it on ourselves.

That's just SO shitty, and so sad.

Thank GOODNESS I had a coach, because as one of my best boos, Jennifer Moore of Modern Medicine Lady, points out to me on a regular basis:

"You can't read the label from inside the jar."

{Side note: this is reason #38,467,896 why you need a mentor, coach, or guide of SOME sort for ANY major undertaking in your life! They can see what you can't from where you're standing, and if they're good, they'll lovingly call you out on it and help you move through it instead of just ducking like you're in a crazed 1980s game of dodgeball}

Because here's what my coach, Joanna, told me: It wasn't that I was terrible with time...*it was that I had WAY too many things on my plate and not enough help.*

{Side note: Interestingly enough, there are deep and fascinating parallels between TIME and MONEY.}

Many people who feel stuck with one ALSO feel stuck with the other.

*In my case, I also had the story that I was TERRIBLE with money (hence not ever feeling like I HAD enough) while Joanna helped me to see that I simply just wasn't MAKING enough for me and the Kid to live on – and I actually performed MIRACLES with what I **did** make, just like I did with my time. See?}*

On a daily basis I was:

* ★ Running on 4-5 hours of sleep
* ★ Taking care of the Kid all day (she'd wake up at 4 am those first few years, and I would get out of work between 11 pm -1 am, so it was a problem)
* ★ Working 5-7 days a week
* ★ Taking care of my dog (my gateway pitbull, Boo Radley. He was the seed of Pittie Posse Rescue, which I'll tell you about later)
* ★ Trying to start a business

Insight Exercise

What are YOU doing on a daily basis?

Make a list of all the things on your plate...as daunting as that might be! You don't have to list every little thing, just the main ones.

★ _____

★ _____

★ _____

★ _____

★ _____

While I began to understand that it wasn't necessarily that I was "bad" with my time – it was that I didn't have enough support – *it still didn't help me figure out how to make everything work for the first few years until I could pay for help, leave the restaurant, etc.*

It didn't help me figure out how to raise this little Kid in as hands-on a way as possible, while also having the time and space I needed to regain my sanity so I could be present with her. Play with her. Laugh. Enjoy her. Spend as much quality time with her as I POSSIBLY could until she reached the age where it wasn't cool to hang out with Mama.

{UPDATE: We're there. She's now 15 and she's as attached to being WITHOUT me as she used to be TO me. BUT... all the time I spent with her when she was younger was SUCH an investment because even at this point where I'm the MOST annoying/least cool person in the universe, she STILL loves spending time with me. We STILL have so much fun together. We're so close. And that might not have been possible if I had kept going the way I was when she was a baby.}

If you're like me, growing your own business is non-negotiable. (What IS negotiable is whether you build yourself a life of freedom or a nicer pair of golden handcuffs.) My business was the life preserver that was being thrown to me (or, that I was throwing to myself) because the way I was living was NOT emotionally or physically sustainable for me, and I wasn't able to be the mama to this precious Kiddo that I wanted to be.

Another factor in the importance of figuring out how to make the time to start my business was that I was working with an immune disorder. I've had the Epstein-Barr virus since I was 19 years old.

Stress, not enough sleep, and crappy eating triggers it and if I don't take care of myself it renders me motionless. When it flares up it brings on either flu-like symptoms or completely incapacitates me for anywhere from a few days to a few weeks. It can completely knock my feet out from under me if I don't take care of myself.

So I REALLY needed a way to set up my time that – SOMEHOW – also gave me time for ME, for rest, and to build back up my peace of mind. I needed to feel like I could raise the Kid, take care of myself, keep our heads above water financially, AND have space to build my new business.

Insight Exercise

What are the things YOU would like to have time for?

Make a list now of the things you need to have time for in your life. Assume your time was your own, just for a moment. What do you NEED? What do you WANT?

★ _____

★ _____

★ _____

★ _____

★ _____

★ _____

★ _____

★ _____

In order to figure out how to *make* this time I needed, I did what most of us do when we need to learn something: I went to Google.

When I googled "time management," I found many, many tools. Many systems. Books, downloadable pdfs, strategies.

SO. MANY. TOOLS.

And yet...NOT A ONE of them was written by a single mama solo-parenting a toddler with a night job, getting 4 hours of sleep a night, who was starting a business.

In fact, *most were created by men.*

I assume that statistically those men who HAD families also had WIVES. And were not juggling solo-parenthood. Or running on 4 hours of sleep per night while they followed toddlers around the playground, juggled dog care, worked every night, and tried not to break down.

None of them were written by multi-passionate, magickal women trying to take over the world and pull it back from the death-grip of the capitalist patriarchy.

None of them were written by mamas with aching hearts who needed to find a way to be present with whatever she was focusing on in the moment. A weepy toddler. A demanding customer. Trying to change the font for HOURS on the damned new website that she was building herself. Trying to BREATHE and not cry through her day.

SO. My need for time management tools, and YOURS, oh-so-normal-probably-middle-to-upper-class-white-man?

--->NOT REALLY THE SAME THING, BUB.<---

Necessity is the mother of invention.

So I created my own damned "time management system."

For mamas.

For healers.

For creative spirits afraid of structure, authority, and rules.

For multi-passionate entrepreneurs who AREN'T willing to sacrifice 80 hours a week to get their work out into the world.

For women who don't accept the spoon-fed notion that we have to CHOOSE which success we want: money or free time? Business success or feeling like a good mama? Sleep or financial stability? Happy clients or happy YOU? Growth or sanity?

BECAUSE THOSE ARE SOME BULLSHIT CHOICES.

I don't accept those choices. I built another way.

And it's been SO successful – not just for me, but for over 15 YEARS of clients – that you're actually here READING this content because I'm sharing it with the WORLD.

I called the tool I built *Sacred Structure* (SS for short), because **it helped me to see time as a container for what I love.**

Instead of it feeling authoritarian or overly structured and restrictive, I chose to think of time as a potential "container" that could provide space for the things I LOVE.

Sacred Structure was the beginning of learning how to BEND TIME: of learning how to have the SAME amount of hours and days as everyone else but DO MORE with them, and FEEL better about my time IN the process...as well as have all the time I want for what I love.

I see Sacred Structure as a freedom-creator. A peace-of-mind-giver. A structure to give me freedom of time to do whatever the hell I want (and still get to everything that needs to get done).

I use Sacred Structure on a day-to-day basis, sure, but it's also a magick wand of a tool for organizing and prioritizing bigger projects and goals.

It's THE tool that allowed me to start and grow In Arms Coaching in 3-4 hours a week those first two years until I was making enough money to quit my night work.

Four years ago I used the tool I'm about to share with you to start something new: a lifelong passion project dream of mine – a pitbull rescue.

At that point I had a 6-figure business, a team of women working for and with me, two tween/teen girls, a wedding coming up, a headstrong puppy, and a new home. My time was FULL.

I had been working in dog rescue as a volunteer for YEARS. I knew the ins and outs of rescue. I could see mistakes other rescues were making that resulted in mismanagement, burn-out for the leaders and volunteers, and even danger for the dogs and the people involved.

But the only model I had of dog rescue was that of a woman (most rescue founders are women) who gave up EVERY-THING in her personal and professional life to rescue dogs.

The rescue workers I had known prioritized rescue over sanity, health, financial stability, intimate and close relationships, and day-to-day enjoyment of life. In general, they weren't super comfortable with people and social interaction. There was drama constantly and many had few close friendships or intimate relationships. **They were ALL exhausted and burnt out** (and I sure as hell know what THAT'S like).

At no point in my life have I been willing to make those sacrifices.

I saw rescue workers become ill from self-neglect, broke from pouring all their money into their rescue, and at the end of their rope emotionally. I saw them turn on each other and create cyber-bullying situations that destroyed rescues – literally causing doors to shut, rescues to close.

At no point did ANY of that feel like an option for me.

I wasn't willing to sacrifice everything in my life to rescue. I wasn't willing to trade my health, relationships, and financial security to rescue. I KNEW that I couldn't be of use to the animals sustainably if I was running on empty myself.

Insight Exercise

What are you NOT willing to sacrifice in the name
of your success?

List your non-negotiables:

★ _____

★ _____

★ _____

★ _____

★ _____

★ _____

★ _____

Like the "Boss Mom/CEO Boss/Hustle" BS, I was angry about that model. I was angry that women (mostly) were losing their LIVES to make a difference for animals.

That model scares a lot of passionate, powerful, magickal women away from their dreams of rescuing animals. It drives a lot of really skilled people from the area. *It creates such massive burnout and compassion fatigue that people don't often survive in rescue very long, or continue at massive personal risk to themselves.*

I want to highlight the fear of what we have to sacrifice to make our dreams happen. Because that's something that's NOT specific to rescue; many of the women who come to me have this fear.

What will "success" cost them? If they grow their business to wealth, what will they have to sacrifice?

We are taught to believe that we can't have it all and be happy, healthy women with rich relationships, peace of mind, and time to do the OTHER things we love.

This stops SO many magickal women from investing in and pursuing their dreams.

That's ONE of the reasons I HAD to get this info to as many women as possible. **I've found a tool to counter these beliefs so you can reach as high as you dream without the fear of what it will cost you.**

This was also my fear and it had kept me from investing in a life-long dream for YEARS: my OWN DOG RESCUE.

Until one business retreat with my coach when I broke down crying over a video I had just seen of a battered, bleeding pitbull named Sal, in a cage at a California shelter.

Blind from blunt head trauma, he was wandering around his cage bumping into walls and barking hysterically with fear and confusion.

He was killed almost immediately.

Sal was a perfect example of a dog that we could have helped. An established, strong rescue could have saved him, gotten love and medical care for him, and given him a chance at a life of love and soft beds.

As I cried sharing this story and my aching heart that wanted to start a rescue but was SO afraid and unwilling to risk everything else in my life, Joanna walked across the room to me and crouched down to look directly into my eyes.

She said, "Normally, you KNOW that I would caution a person about how much can be on their plate, and how many different focal points they can hold SUCCESSFULLY. But this time, it's different.

"You NEED to do this. You need to start your rescue. And I know you can do it."

So after our wedding, on the way up to a long weekend in Bar Harbor I pitched the idea to my brand-new husband, Sully, and because that's the kind of guy he is, he was all in immediately.

It was late September of 2016.

Sacred Structure allowed me to prioritize the first few steps and make a timeline, and then sit with my calendar and start shaping the time I was going to need to get Pittie Posse Rescue off the ground.

Because of Sacred Structure and the tools it's given me, within 6 months we had an official 501(c) 3 non-profit organization with a small team of volunteers who were on board to open the metaphorical doors with us.

Four years later, we've saved over 400 dogs. We have a team of 10 almost-full-time volunteer coordinators, and we save dogs from Georgia, New Mexico, and Maine.

My day-to-day now includes:

* ★ Running and growing In Arms Coaching, supporting team and clients
* ★ Running and growing Pittie Posse Rescue and its new pet food pantry and supporting my coordinators and volunteers
* ★ Managing the hormonal, emotional, and physical needs of two teen girls
* ★ The care of 4 pitbulls and 9 chickens
* ★ The growth and maintenance of a marriage
* ★ A few good, deep friendships with the women I love
* ★ My own self-evolution: courses, study, magickal work, reading as many books as I can, meditation, and self-reflection
* ★ And my own care and well-being, with LOTS of time to be outdoors in the beautiful nature of Maine
* ★ AND...by the time this book is in your hands, the launching of a THIRD business – a joint passion project between Sully and myself

Insight Exercise

Looking ahead into the future you are working towards, what would your ideal day-to-day include (be as specific as you like)?

★ _____

★ _____

★ _____

★ _____

★ _____

★ _____

★ _____

I could NOT have made my ideal days happen without Sacred Structure.

And I know I can help you make it work for YOU, too.

Why Sacred Structure and Who Is It For?

I'm a woman's woman.

I believe in us.

I love us.

If I could live in a community of JUST women, I would (my husband feels similarly, and often tries to slip into my women's events as an "honorary woman.").

My heart belongs to women. When I look back over my adult life, I've constantly gravitated towards supporting women, loving women, helping women heal, and working to guide and support more of us into POWER: in our lives, our communities, our businesses, and the world. It's been a part of my vision for my whole adult life.

I believe the MOTHER-FUCKING antidote to the supreme FUCKERY we're experiencing right now is WOMEN leading the way, and men moving to the back to take a seat.

The patriarchal model of leadership and the men who have held so many positions of power throughout the history of this country have FUCKED it all up, and now it's time to let us take the reins and try to fix their mess.

I believe in the matriarchal/feminine model of leadership.

I believe in collaboration over competition.

I believe in human rights: in every human's entitlement to a safe home, clean water to drink, medical support when they need it, and access to safe work that pays a living wage.

I believe in magick.

I believe in prioritizing nature and the environment as the mother-fricking LUNGS, heart, and soul of our world.

I believe in being the voice for the voiceless. Animal rights. Children's rights.

The rights of mothers to not have to CHOOSE between being a present, loving mama with her own oxygen mask on and putting fricking FOOD on the table.

I believe in communities surrounding and supporting single mamas, and each OTHER.

That's a short list of what I believe in, but I know that when women are in power, when we control the purse strings, the courtrooms, the policies and laws being made...

Things are going to change from the collectively-suicidal path we're on now.

---> AND...I know from almost 15 years of experience that the key to the tides changing is us having the time, sanity, and our oxygen mask on to be able to DO the work we're called to do. To feel supported.<---

I needed Sacred Structure and it didn't exist. I struggled until I created it, and now I can just apply it and reapply it anytime I add something new into my life.

How you spend your time is the difference between creating the life you want and unintentionally building a trap for yourself in the pursuit of the freedom you desire.

If you're not carefully creating conscious boundaries and clear focus with your time...your dreams, work, and vision will spiral into a day-to-day blur of BUSY that turns into the opposite of what you wanted for yourself.

Insight Exercise

What aspects of the life you are living now feel like a trap?

What areas have blurry boundaries (or downright non-existent ones)?

What 'seemed like a good idea at the time' but just isn't working anymore?

★ _____

★ _____

★ _____

★ _____

★ _____

★ _____

You CAN succeed AND have a personal life.

You have found me and Sacred Structure just in the nick of time if you're living in a blur of busy-ness with no space for quiet, reflection, rest, or relaxation. If you have no time to water the roots of what you're growing, or what you want to grow. If so far it's all just flying by while you flail to keep your head above water.

When you're existing in survival mode with only enough time to work IN your business, your dreams suffer. Your energy suffers. Your focus suffers.

Your magick suffers. You can't focus your energy clearly to make what you want HAPPEN.

And I, personally, have a DEEP investment in YOUR magic, m'kay? I'm invested in a world where women are supported in being as powerful, happy, and healthy as they can possibly be.

This is the vision I have for the world that I want to hand over to my daughter.

NOW is the moment to own your time and feel GOOD about how you're spending it, in all areas of your life.

On the path to lucrative work that you love, that brings you visibility, a healthy income, and the impact that you want to be having in the world, WHILE you nurture your physical, spiritual, and emotional self. This is a road that is ticking with land mines that can derail you – for days, or even completely.

I want to help you walk the path without detonating the land mines that blow you off course or stop you in your tracks.

I want your path to feel like a glorious, tree-lined, light-speckled wandering through a lush forest, teeming with flowers and moss and the occasional deer and rabbits to delight you!

Here's a bit of a controversial position in the professional world, but it's mine, and I'm standing by it:

Sinking ALL your time, energy, and effort into your biz is ultimately a mistake.

I'll say more about that in a minute...BUT, for now, let's acknowledge that when you need your business to succeed, it seems to make sense to do that.

Take it from someone who's pushed herself until she broke: it really doesn't have to be that way. And, if you're anything like me, it actually CAN'T be that way.

Who Needs Sacred Structure?

* ★ Multi-passionate women entrepreneurs who need time for more than one focus

* ★ Women business owners who want to build success without sacrificing personal time, sanity, or peace of mind

* ★ Creative women who want to get their work into the world

* ★ Activists and leaders who need to balance passion work with personal life and have the focus and sanity to make an impact

* ★ Women who need time and space to be magickal AND impactful. To be focused and structured but also creative and inspired

* ★ Women who buck the idea of "structure" (but might paradoxically work better with the RIGHT structure),

externally imposed rules, and feeling "scheduled" but also know they need a way to focus on ALL their heart's desires

★ Mamas who want to feel focused on being present with their kids when they're with them (and not guilty about not working) and focused on their work when they're working (and not guilty about not being with the kids)

★ Witches, healers, artists who need to find focus, structure, and effective work habits but also don't want to feel like they're stuck in "corporate" or "normal" day schedules

★ Women who get stuck in procrastination and overwhelm when trying to get focused and move ahead

★ Women who feel they "fail" at "managing" their time

★ Women who are trying to move towards goals but don't know quite what to "DO" when they have "time to work"

★ New entrepreneurs or business owners who are not sure how to juggle time spent IN their biz, time spent ON their biz, and time checked OUT of their biz

★ ^^^That's a short list, BTW :-)

In summary, I'm so glad that you're here.

In Her Own Words: Jessica

"Before I learned Sacred Structure I had very few time blocks in my calendar. Most of them were for client sessions and the rest of my time was unstructured.

I am highly intuitive and used to believe that I loved unstructured time most of the time.

But SS showed me that I was out of balance and not as in control of my time as I had thought, which led to symptoms of overwhelm and anxiety. I was lacking self-care and putting work and other responsibilities before myself.

I was at risk of continuing the pattern of overwhelm and BURNOUT. I realized there were so many things that I had been wanting to do but could not get to them. I thought I either didn't have enough time or I was too burnt out to add something else to my plate. I realized that the way I was managing my time was keeping stuck, tired, and lacking excitement in my life.

It affected my business. A program that was set up to help me reach my income goal never got promoted and got pushed off...which left me not reaching the income goal that I knew was possible.

Sacred Structure taught me to identify what was really important to me at the time while knowing that it can change (I love that part – I love knowing that my calendar is a living and breathing organism that changes and grows with me). SS also helped take off the pressure and helped me really dial in to what mattered.

Britt's stories about her own process in developing sacred structure and also the history of women's struggle to balance work and personal priorities helped to begin to release the guilt and shame so that I could implement SS.

I am now much more in control of my schedule. I understand my priorities and carve out time each week for them. That means I have the time for myself, my family, and my work in a way that feels good for me. I've learned to have a lot less guilt and more compassion for myself. I can be more present for myself, my family, and my business and clients. And I still have the spontaneous, free time that I love without the fear of burnout or guilt.

All of which helped me create a new program that I am totally excited about! I was able to roll it out easily and begin to enroll women into it. I can see the potential of its growth and how it will help me reach my income goals.

I have way more time in my life than I've had in the past to not only grow my business but to take care of myself and spend time with my family. And I now recommend SS to the women I work with.

If you are looking for a successful tool to help you utilize your time, DIVE IN. It is so worth it. You deserve the tools Britt teaches so that you can gain control of your time and feel better!"

—Jessica Kaloutas, North Shore Myofascial Release

Chapter 2

The Resistance

Bottom line, Boo: It doesn't matter how successful you are...if you're spending your time in ways you don't enjoy, that don't line up with what you really want in life...

If you're not doing what you love most of the time, then ultimately you will get to a place where *even if you create "success,"* **the money you make isn't worth what you've sacrificed to make it.**

AND: the overwhelm, exhaustion, and distraction from spending your time in ways that don't match your heart-centered priorities will cause you to lose your connection with yourself, your magick, and your passion. They will DISCONNECT you from your heart, your third eye, your source of wisdom and your connection to All That Is.

Imagine a life where you're NOT exhausted, overwhelmed, and constantly busy, juggling a million demands. Imagine a life where you are the queen of your schedule, the duchess of down-time, where you wake up every day LOOKING FORWARD to living your everyday life.

This connection is where your magick comes from, and an attachment to it is necessary to fill your cup, connect you to a source of your energy, and access your intuition and power on a sustainable basis.

THE severing of you from yourself is arguably an intentional result of the capitalist patriarchal mentality.

And we're not having it.

It's done us too much harm.

It's time for us to wake up.

To ourselves.

To each other.

It's time for leadership to be Heart-Led, instead of Greed-Led.

I DO *firmly believe that the above is an actual* INTENTION *and* CONSTRUCT *of the Toxic Patriarchy. The patriarchal order was actually* BUILT *to keep bitches like us* DOWN. *Disempowered. Chasing our tails.*

{*Side Note: A word on the use of the phrase "toxic patriarchy."*}

If you're worried or feel like I'm bashing men...I'm not AT ALL.

The toxic patriarchy is NOT about men. *There are many men I love, admire, am inspired by, and hell, I sleep next to one at night. It would be rough at home if I thought he sucked because he's a man.*

The term refers to toxic traits attributed to masculinity that don't serve men, either, such as:

- hypermasculine culture (machismo, showing off, hypercompetitiveness)

- cult of force (despising "the weak," "the immature," "the ill," etc.)

- ethic of violence and warfare, domination and suppression of difference/foreignness

- abuse of women, children, animals and the natural world, domination over them, disregarding their rights and treating them as inferior, as slaves or servants, whose fate is to serve the predominantly male social structures. (Pechenyak, What is the toxic patriarchy? 2019)

Cuz know what? Our great, great, great grandmothers? WERE POWERFUL AF.

They were SO powerful, magickal, and connected that it was HARD when homeboys started raising the roofs of institutions such as, and in particular, the church and the institution of medicine (both of which women were prohibited from participating in as leaders).

Our Great-Great-Greats were a HUGE P.I.T.A. (pain in the ass) because they were effective as all hell with the spiritual, emotional, and physical needs of their communities.

People TRUSTED them, and our Greats helped their people. Nobody WANTED to abandon them and start trusting the church and the new doctors – who, by the way were all MEN because, again, women weren't ALLOWED access to being considered "hands of God" and practitioners of institutional medicine.

WE ARE THE
granddaughters
of the witches
YOU COULDN'T **BURN.**

We are of the new world order (it's actually the OLD world order, but you know what I mean – we're here for the mother-fricking REBIRTH), where we don't sacrifice pieces of ourselves to be in leadership. We don't accept the disconnect. We don't buy the idea that financial stability and doing the work we love has to come at the price of our personal lives.

We believe that we are NEEDED. That our work is necessary. That the more centered, focused, and WOKE we are, the more change we can create.

We KNOW that the world NEEDS OUR CHANGE.

We believe that our power comes from us, WHOLE. Intact. Unified. Well-fed. Rested. Laughter-filled.

Are you with me?

We have been fed some seriously damaging myths when it comes to how we spend our time. (You've been reminded of WHY, above.)

These myths have the power to derail your whole life and your biz, one lost day at a time.

One such myth is the following. See if this resonates for you: the myth that there will be time "later" for the change you want NOW.

Like: "I'll sleep more LATER. I'll learn to meditate LATER, when things are calmer. I'll put myself first when work slows down. I'll take full weekends off/unplug for a day or two at a time/go for long walks every morning with my kid when _____."

What most people fail to notice is that today IS yesterday's "later."

Later never actually comes. Because when it gets here it becomes "now" and that's the perfect time to put whatever it is off again until later.

Now is all we have, Magickal One.

Insight Exercise

What have YOU been putting off until later? *What are the results of you putting these things off?*

★ _____

★ _____

★ _____

★ _____

★ _____

★ _____

★ _____

One of the premises of alchemical work is that you have to start where you stand.

You have to start with you.

That change you want to see – for yourself, in yourself, or perhaps even for everyone in the world – that change has to start right now.

With today.

It has to start RIGHT where you stand.

It might happen one tiny bit at a time (which I'll talk about later) but it has to start with doing something different – this is the key to actually creating different results than the ones you've managed to experience so far.

This belief, in particular, shows up frequently for my clients around hiring team and support staff.

There's the fear that you have to wait until there's lots of extra money to hire – and I can tell you two things from more than 15 years' experience:

1. It's hard to get to a point where it FEELS like we have "enough" money. It's always going to be tempting to put off investing in yourself and your business.

2. Unless you get support you will quickly hit a point in your business where your lack of support is actually COSTING you money. It's tricky because you're going to have to SPEND a little money to see it, but with any business or work that's starting to gain traction, you'll see that without support either you're doing EVERYTHING in your business, even the things that aren't your brilliance, or you're not great at, or you hate so they take you FOREVER (OR YOU JUST WIND UP NOT DOING THEM), or you max out on hours in your day, and don't have any more TIME to make more money because you're doing everything: the work you love, yes, but also the admin work. The cleaning. The cooking. Pet care. Childcare. The financials and accounting and billing. Client care. Seriously – if you're here, look at how many different

team members it would take to do what you have on your plate in an average week.

In my programs for women entrepreneurs and business owners, we have a system for untangling this tangle for our clients.

We start with a first step, like getting clear around the fear and beliefs around hiring a team.

We sort out what's actually being done, what balls are getting dropped, and whom would be the most essential person to bring on board within the next 3 months, then 6 months out, then next year.

We then build support and team slowly, carefully, with no quick, jarring movements or expenses...but it's INCREDIBLE the results that my clients feel IMMEDIATELY, even at the very beginning of the process.

Another common myth is the belief that when you finally become "successful," THAT'S when you get to enjoy your time. My first coach, Joanna, calls this "the myth of arrival."

There's so much wrong with that statement that I barely know where to start. But I will say that it connects to the first myth of "Later." **This is a slippery slope of a belief that feeds disconnect from the present moment** and primes your brain to be expecting what it needs at some future point (that very well might never come, by the way).

One of the expectations that I want you to build while reading this book is that **you can start enjoying your life now, IF you know how to structure it**.

Read that again.

I don't want you to wait for some unicorn-filled, mythical future point where everything will magickally fall into place and you'll be happy and at peace.

Actually, here's what I want to say: you MUST start enjoying your life in the here and now, instead of waiting for a mythical time that actually isn't even a thing. **Dammit, let's make THAT happen, m'kay?**

Working the way I'm going to show you in this book will also magickally speed up your path to other kinds of success in your:

★ Health

★ Relationships

★ Parenting, if you're doing that sort of thing

★ In your friendships

Insight Exercise

List the areas of your life you'd like to be successful in.
What would that success look like in each area?

★ _____

★ _____

★ _____

★ _____

★ _____

★ _____

★ _____

Spending your time and life doing the things you love now is the main kind of success most of us are interested in anyway.

Let's talk about what doesn't work in terms of time management and why.

It's probably going to sound very familiar, and that's good because the more you can SEE what doesn't work, the more you can love it up and accept it, so it stops sabotaging you.

It's really important to look at what isn't working or hasn't worked for you in the past, because what HASN'T worked is a goldmine of info that'll give you crucial perspective on where you've gotten stuck before.

The reason you haven't found peace with your time, the reason you don't feel in control of your time, or whatever brought you to this book, isn't about a LACK OF RESOURCES. There are a JILLION time management strategies out there. You've probably tried many of them :-)

I do feel confident that my tools are going to resonate more for you if you're a magickal biz owner, or multi-passionate woman entrepreneur, because we have more in common than you do with the people who created many of the other tools out there...BUT, it's absolutely crucial to ALSO start by looking at where YOUR blocks are around your time.

I will give you powerful, hard-and-fast tools for being in control of your time and ensuring there's space for everything you love (because what you pay attention to and feed grows), but ALSO to lead you to understanding what's stood in your way of the above up until now.

Most of that is going to actually be within YOU: in your beliefs, patterns, and fears. We're going to begin to dig into that so you can see it clearly and work with it (obviously we can't do ALL the work in this short book).

Earlier I spoke about the common misconception many of us start off with: that to build biz success you have to sacrifice the rest of your life, which is based largely on a historical male-dominated model.

Women's general refusal to spend most of our time working is something that sets us apart from our male biz owner counterparts.

We want success, but most of us, myself included, are NOT willing to work 80-90 hours a week. Even if we did that, most of us would also STILL be in charge of our home, or pets, or kids, or social life, etc.

The work in this book is one of the VERY first steps that I lead ALL my clients through – because your time is the most valuable thing you have. **Once you learn to structure it around what you love most and your highest priorities, everything's going to change, including your focus and energy.**

By the end of this book, **you'll** have a container for how to spend your time that allows you to build your biz AND have time for the other things you need and want to do, INCLUDING time for you, which is SOOOO important.

Let's talk for a minute about that **busy-ness addiction** that we collectively have as a culture. To some degree or another, this impacts your beliefs around time and how "productive" or busy you are.

The "Cult of Busy," as I call it, hands out badges for "who runs around the most like a chicken with its head cut off." We compare notes about how crazy busy we are. It's a freaky, twisted badge of honor. It's almost like we believe that if we're NOT so busy we're about to cry we might not DESERVE success, or income, or support…

But the Cult of Busy is an incredibly harmful club to belong to. It creates a neural pathway to constant multi-tasking, which is a highly addictive and difficult-to-break practice.

I'm inviting you right now to reconsider with every fiber of your being your attachment to "busyness" and if you are willing to forge a different, more peaceful and fulfilling path.

If you are ready, let's make it official:

I, _____ (your name), am willing to release my membership in the Cult of Busyness in exchange for the life I actually want.

_____
Your signature

Ready to make it real?
Repeat the above statement aloud a few times a day in front of a mirror.

Speaking is powerful magick – did you know that the phrase "Abracadabra" actually means: "I will create as I speak?" More about that later.

Feeling like you don't have enough time or not being clear about how you spend it leads to stressing and multi-tasking, both of which actually cost MORE energy and keep your brain from being able to deeply focus, which is when it's at its most effective.

You end up doing LESS while it's costing you MORE energy, which means you don't have the energy you need to go full steam in your biz.

Additionally, multi-tasking has you switching mental gears haphazardly, which means you're not being EFFECTIVE at ANY of the things you're doing.

In the end it takes twice as much time and energy to get half as much accomplished than if you could sit and focus in a laser-like way on one task at a time.

Multi-tasking rewires your brain in a way that costs you peace of mind and the ability to hone in on one thing at a time and be PRESENT, or feel focused. Which means no matter what you're getting done, your time won't FEEL good, and ultimately YOU won't feel good.

I used to subscribe to the "Cult of Busy."

"Busy" felt like a badge of honor. I used to bond via stressing with other women – and I won't lie, it made me feel needed, necessary, and even kind of important.

It was hard to create moments of peace and groundedness and operate from that place, and I couldn't understand why. I didn't WANT to feel "crazy," but it was oddly compelling. It was hard to break out of it. One year, at a business retreat with my coach, I realized why.

Being "busy," or "overwhelmed," is a highly addictive behavior for your brain and body. It trains your brain and body to become dependent on stress hormones for fuel, which feeds a cycle of relying on running around like a chicken without its head to get things done.

As someone with finite reserves of energy due to immune disorders, depleted adrenals, etc., I realized that when I really stopped to feel into it, my attachment to constantly being SO BUSY was, in part, because I believed that if I stopped my breakneck speed, I'd crash.

My energy to keep moving came from franticness/stress. It wasn't really "energy" as much as it was an adrenaline rush that I began to rely on to keep moving. It cost me my adrenal functioning, which I'm STILL trying to nurse back to health, years later.

We're secretly afraid that adrenaline is ALL that keeps us moving. We come to rely on panic and stress to help us focus and move forward. We forget how to motivate ourselves and access energy without it. We're afraid that if we don't keep moving, we'll drop.

Additionally, the "busy-ness" makes us feel productive. It makes us feel a little important and needed. It gives us a connecting point to bitch about, helping us bond with other women who are doing the same thing.

It also contributes to our feelings of worthiness and deserving. We MUST deserve the success we experience, because – LOOK – WE ARE KILLING OURSELVES for it.

This is a toe-dip into something we're going to spend some time on further on: the inner pieces of time management for women like us.

Because being a successful biz owner requires that you learn how to be a witch. Let me explain what I mean by that.

Tattooed across my right arm is the phrase, "Abracadadabra." You definitely know this phrase if you've seen *Sesame Street*!

As I mentioned a few pages ago, "Abracadabra" is actually an old Aramaic phrase meaning, "I create as I speak."

It is a powerful reminder that **our words are energetic tools** that create our perspective, which shapes our experience of what's happening. That, in turn, dictates the results we achieve.

Magick is about changing your energy.

I teach my clients how to change the way you think in order to change the way you feel. Changing the way you perceive things is absolutely the beginning of changing the way you experience them.

And that's a REALLY big deal.

When you can *choose* your response to events, situations, and emotional states of mind, instead of feeling stuck and caught in REACTING to them, you are empowered to DECIDE the action you want to take. That can drastically change not JUST the results of your actions, but also the way YOU feel as you're creating those results – whether they're the results you planned for, or not.

Claiming ownership is a crucial component of the journey I take my clients on. Ownership means that while you don't take responsibility for everything that happens to you, you take responsibility for your REACTION to it. That's big, right there. It's also a really important piece of true leadership – moving from reacting to responding.

Ready to get started? Let's do some pulse-taking.

Note: If you'd prefer a pretty worksheet that I made for you to actually print out and use, just go to the bonus page of resources I want you to have: *https://InArmsCoaching.com/bookfreegift*

Pulse-taking

Begin by thinking about where you are in your biz and writing your answers to the following questions:

- ★ What's happening (and maybe more importantly not happening) because you're not able to own your time and spend it the way you want to?

- ★ What's not working for you about the way you spend your time these days: biz and personal?

- ★ How is this affecting your biz? How is it affecting how your DAY feels? How is that affecting the rest of your life?

- ★ What are your top 3 goals for your biz in this next year?

- ★ What kind of support do you have in place to ensure you meet those goals?

- ★ Does the way you spend your time align with those goals, or not? Explain.

(Don't worry if your answer is that it really doesn't. What we're doing next will help with that. We're just finding your starting point, which is always really important to know.)

What does this mean?

- ★ What do you notice from the work above?

- ★ What's not working, and how does it hold you back from your goals?

- ★ What's the impact on your personal life of spending your time this way?

- ★ What pieces of self-care, spiritual, personal, or physical is suffering because of the way your time is spent right now?

- ★ And how is it squashing or impeding your ability to do the work and magick you're called to do?

Focus-Pocus

One of my favorite quotes is:

> *"If you don't know what you want, you have little to NO chance of getting it."*

(NO *idea where it came from. Joanna said it to me, I think, a few times, YEARS ago, but didn't quote the source and I have been unable to find it. But I think it's awesome and I use it frequently.*)

In the TV series Sons of Anarchy (season 2, episode 6), the matriarch of SOA, Gemma, teaches Tara (her son's partner), how to shoot a gun.

(*When you're a bad-ass partner of a seriously HOT, murderous biker, this is apparently a skill you need to master. Makes sense to me.*)

She shows Tara how to hold the weapon. How to focus on the target until she sees nothing else. How to aim, take a big breath, and steadily pull the trigger.

Like shooting to kill (*but maybe let's think of it as KILL-ING your goals instead of a human being...*), you have to be **focused on your goal, grounded in your body, and have all your energy pointed towards your target with as little distraction as possible.**

How does this apply to time management?

In order to move forward in owning your time and making sure ALL your energy is pointed in the right direction, you first need to understand where your foot is metaphorically on the brake. **You need to see clearly and remove any place where your energy is unfocused or resistant to what you say you want.**

Having the mental equivalent of your foot on the brake means you're losing energy, instead of knowing how to focus your energy exactly where you want it to go, without scattering it, feeling lost, or getting bogged down in overwhelm.

In the magickal practice that I use, the first part of making change is about the SOLVE aspect of alchemy.

Solve (pronounced SOL-vay) is the alchemical practice of dissolving something for the purpose of getting its essence and re-using or applying it to get something MORE desirable down the road.

In this context, solve is used to find your resistance, your blocks, your fears and conflicting desires, and dissolve them into something that you can use to build a clear focus and path to your goals.

This is why it's crucial to start by flushing out the reasons why time isn't ALREADY working for you.

It may sound weird, but if you don't have time management skills that work for you yet, **there's likely a deeper reason why your time isn't working for you**, in addition to just not being able to find an aligned tool.

If you don't see this part clearly – WHAT gets in the WAY of you feeling in control of your time – then you'll just keep trying tool after tool, none of them really having any lasting effect on your success.

Let's start with this analogy: Imagine that you get in your car to SPEED to an appointment (because you're late, because, well, TIME...).

You jam your foot on the gas and prepare to fly forward down the road.

But nothing happens...because your LEFT foot is on the BRAKE pedal.

You don't get the forward motion that you need because you're trying to take two opposing actions at one time, and they cancel themselves out (and break your vehicle).

{*Side note: NYC cab drivers use this technique in traffic all the time. It's terrifying, results in a constant jerking movement, and probably destroys their vehicles, as well as earning them a horrible reputation as drivers. Don't be a NYC cab driver.*}

Becoming sovereign over your time is NOT just a matter of learning the "right" time management tool. If that were the case, you'd have, like, 6 gad-jillion different superficial strategies out there to choose from.

There are deeper, inner pieces that block your ability to use your time the way you really want to, the way you know intrinsically would work best for you.

And without seeing those clearly and working with them in the light of day where they're visible...

LIKELY, no amount of time management tools is REALLY going to change the way you spend your time, OR...

How you FEEL about your time.

This is where the magick comes in. :-)

My working definition of magick (and the way I teach it in my programs) is the art and science of changing your energy.

That's the kind of magick we do when we work together.

SIDE NOTE: *Why I use the spelling "magick" instead of "magic." The addition of the "k" is from controversial occultist Aleister Crowley – the founder of the religion of Thelema (from the Greek word meaning "Will") and leader of the British occult movement and spiritual practice that became known as Wicca.*

While Mr. Crowley was not a particularly awesome human being, (in fact, he was pretty douchey – by many accounts a truly shitty person) he was a brilliant occultist.

He changed the spelling for several reasons – one was to distinguish the concept of Magick from the parlor tricks of "magic" to set it apart as work that brings us closer to our true will, or purpose, in life. He taught that in order to effect outer change in the world (like, with magick), you first had to examine, know, and change your INNER world – your thoughts, beliefs, and patterns of thinking.

So I use the extra "k" as a signifier that we're not just talking about the historically "woo" parts of new age magic: the crystals, sage, affirmations, etc. Those are nice too, but real MAGIC-with-a-K is about looking inwards for the answers and getting support from other realms to change the way you think and act in order to achieve your true calling, goals, and will.

Let me tell you something REALLY cool about you. I hope you already know this, but even if you do, sometimes it's nice to hear someone else say it:

You are REALLY, really powerful.

Like, you probably don't run around in Wonder Woman's get-up, but you're CRAZY powerful, just like she is (you don't even NEED the cool cuffs – that's how crazy amazing you are).

Most of us didn't have her upbringing (but who wants an amaza-balls island of bad-ass women to mentor and teach you??? ME!!! I DO!!!!), so instead of learning to USE our power we were actually taught to hide it, disconnect from it, and have fear/shame about it.

That's REALLY heartbreaking.

It happened to me. And I'm betting that in some way, shape, or form, it happened to you.

Through late childhood and my teen years I self-destructed, abused myself, and put myself in dangerous and abusive situations because of this severing. *I've spent most of my adult life working to help women connect back with their power and learn to use it.*

As women we are discouraged from understanding how to use our magick in areas such as getting visible so the world can see you and what you offer and snatch it up, so that you can become financially sovereign, so that you can call relationships into your life that are healthy and nurturing and supportive...

{WHICH ARE ALL built around knowing how to feel sovereign with your time...}

We are discouraged as children by being told (sometimes by well-meaning adults who, themselves, were told the same things) to be quieter. Not to boast. To let others have a chance before us. To not intimidate others. To not take up too much space. We were made to feel responsible for the actions and thoughts of others. We were taught to consider other people's feelings and comfort before our own.

I don't care where you grew up, in what religion or culture, or how loving your parents were: the universal culture of toxic masculinity and the resulting disempowerment of women and girls affected your brain development via parental guidance, family culture, ceilings on achievement, family stories about achievement and beliefs, the ways you were treated in schools, media and the advertising culture, and the religious and political oppression of women the world over.

It's a universal system of oppression, misogyny, and detachment from our inner wisdom and power that none of us have completely escaped.

We bring it with us into our visions, work, and aspirations.

It's not our fault. It's inescapable to some degree in our culture.

In part, because of this, there are barriers that you (we all) put up to slow down success, balance, happiness, and prosperity so that we toe the line and blend in with the people around us.

Let's take a look at some of the most common.

Most of us have what Carolyn Elliot, of WITCH, calls "Divided Will" around the things we say we want.

> *This means that while your conscious brain wants something, your subconscious brain actually has a fear, block, or belief that is the OPPOSITE of what your conscious mind wants.*

Here are some examples.

> Example: Your conscious mind wants to make WAY more money.
>
> Your unconscious mind is terrified of getting in trouble with the IRS, paying WAY more taxes, pissing off or intimidating our friends who have less income, being asked for money by our family, being accused of being a fraud, sell out, or greedy capitalist, etc.
>
> Example: Your conscious mind wants to attract new clients easily, like moths to a light.
>
> Your unconscious mind is uncomfortable with visibility. It's afraid of attracting trolls, being accused of boasting, being too big for your britches, having so many clients that your time and sanity is compromised, not having enough time for your kids, being judged for your POV or philosophy or beliefs.

See the push and pull happening behind the scenes?

See how it can SEEM like you're pointed at a desire and goal, but there's actually a big, powerful part of your brain that has its foot on the brake?

Bottom line: what you THINK you want is complicated. If it's not happening, there's likely more than one reason why, and you might not be seeing it clearly (which means you're helpless against it).

If, for instance, you want to be internationally known for the work you do so that the right customers or clients flock to you, credit card in hand...

Then you need to be visible.

And being visible is scary for women. You might offend or anger people. You might attract internet trolls who attack you publicly. People might accuse you of being a fraud or taking up too much space, because surely there are other people in your field who know more or have been doing this longer.

So working to be VISIBLE is alluring, necessary, and desirable...but ALSO scary, intimidating, and uncomfortable. You have reasons why you want it, and you ALSO have reasons (of which you might not be conscious yet) why you DON'T want it.

Insight Exercise

For each area where you desire success,

list what you fear about attaining that success.

★ _____

★ _____

★ _____

★ _____

★ _____

★ _____

Do you want to be financially stable with savings, investments, debt paid off, and money to do the things that make you happy?

Then you need to build your work to the point where you and your clients DEEPLY value the expertise you carry and you charge healthy rates and make wise financial decisions.

Claiming your expertise, being wealthy, learning to make wise financial decisions, investing in yourself...all those can be uncomfortable and triggering.

You probably have old beliefs and fears about what it means to be really wealthy.

About claiming healthy rates for the work you do.

About what people will think of you if you have no debt and money in the bank.

Maybe there's pride attached to your struggle, or the triumphing over financial hardship.

Maybe you have fear about being taken advantage of, around taking responsibility for others if you have lots of money, or fear of what your family of origin will think of you.

So while financial stability and abundance may be deeply desirable, it can also be charged with fear and discomfort.

That's Divided Will.

I guarantee you that if you're reading this book looking for time management tools that'll work for you because none have so far, it's more complicated for you than just not having found the right tool yet.

These are just a couple of examples but the results of them both require that you understand how to be in control of your time in order to get what you want. You can also see clearly in both examples why you might have an investment in NOT reaching the goals you say you want. Yes?

Can you see why you might have Divided Will about mastering time and feeling sovereign about the goals you want?

Let's come back to what I said in the first part of this book: **When you're building your own biz, there's often a fear or belief about what success would COST you.**

Stop for a second and feel that out for yourself. Is there a belief, however big or small, yours OR handed to you, *that you'll have to settle or compromise in order to have a successful, money-making biz?*

What are you afraid you might need to compromise in order to have, build, or create what you dream of?

Examples of some limiting beliefs might be:

* ★ I don't have time for the things I love
* ★ I can't afford to spend time doing what I love
* ★ It's impossible for me to structure my days according to what I love most
* ★ I'm too busy/disorganized/unskilled at this to put what I love at the center of my days
* ★ If I spend time doing what I love, I won't have enough $ to live
* ★ No one will pay me to do what I love

Write down any of the above that feel applicable, and add your own.

Insight Exercise

What stories do you tell yourself about creating structure in your life? About managing your time? About having room for the things that you love?

★ _____

★ _____

★ _____

★ _____

★ _____

★ _____

One of the first steps you want to look at when you want to change a result you're getting is: what do you already HAVE in process? What's working? What isn't?

This is all SO important to see, because unless you're really cognizant about what's scary, uncomfortable, or worrisome about having what you want, you can work as hard as you can on creating it but STILL have an unconscious foot on the brake when trying to make it happen.

Ready? It's on.

Chapter 3

Outing Myself

I'm going to out myself – I used to be THE MOST STUB-BORN, MOST "avoiding-planning-person" EVER.

I had a juicy NUMBER of reasons that I didn't want to/ couldn't/wouldn't plan.

For one thing, I thought that I wasn't capable of planning.

Actually, my fear was more that I didn't STICK to plans once I made them, so planning just meant failure. It meant one more instance of setting myself up to not follow through with something. And then feeling shitty and shameful.

I also worried that planning would cramp my creativity and any sense of spontaneity, and my day would feel misaligned, full of drudgery, and devoid of inspiration. I wouldn't feel FREE. **I HATE me some authority**, and that's what I worried that STRUCTURE and "a schedule" would feel like.

But what I noticed as I moved forward was that while I was technically making it "work" without planning, struc-ture, and a clear schedule, I was NOT getting the results I wanted. That meant I was earning less than I wanted to be earning – which, oddly, felt LESS like "freedom" than I thought it would.

My commitment to flying by the seat of my pants meant that launches fell flat, programs started without as many women as I wanted, financial goals went unmet, and I spent way more hours struggling than I wanted. I was actually aiming for NO hours spent struggling, so there was THAT...

I began to connect the dots: my definition of "freedom" was less about "no rules" or structure and was actually more about sovereignty.

sov·er·eign·ty
/ˈsäv(ə)rən(t)ē/

A supreme authority... the right of something or someone to govern themselves. It's when you're your own mother-trucking, self-governing STATE or entity...

I wanted to feel in control of my time AND my finances. I wanted to decide when I worked and for how much. I wanted to earn enough money to feel abundant and be able to make my own choices about how we lived. Where we lived. With whom we lived.

Paradoxically, I was beginning to wonder if there was a structure and schedule that would allow me to CREATE my own version of freedom, but first I had to give up my attachment to flying by the seat of my pants and calling THAT freedom.

That's when I went out on a limb and I did something that Joanna had been asking me to do for YEARS (that's how stubborn I was). I PLANNED THE NEXT YEAR OUT.

And...DAMMIT...that was the year that my biz hit 6 figures. That was the first year that there was MORE money than I needed to live on.

Planning everything out allowed me to leverage my time. Work ahead of the crunch and deadlines. Ask for help and delegate. The content I put out looked better, worked better, and gave myself enough TIME for the strategy that would allow more women access to it, which overjoyed me.

The results were awesome enough for me to not kick myself TOO hard for spending all those years resisting the very work that would make my time work for ME, instead of me working for IT.

NOTE: It wasn't as simple as JUST laying out a blueprint and planning my strategy according to my goal.

I also had to look at the inner pieces, or where my foot was on the brake: what was uncomfortable about planning. What was scary about success, fear of failure, etc. This was the REAL meat of why I had gotten so stuck around planning and effectively using my time. My biz coach was crucial in that deep-digging work.

This is the same for EVERY woman I work with.

It's not that we can't find or learn how to use the tools. It's that we have beliefs, fears, and stories that prevent us from getting out of our own way.

CASE STUDY: Crystal

Crystal came to me after years of orbiting in my larger groups and offerings.

She was incredibly skilled at what she did, so much so that she could – and WOULD – book herself SOLID.

And by SOLID, I mean that when we first started working together and I asked her to sketch out her day for me, it was literally "work from waking to sleeping." She worked 6-7 days a week. She was a machine.

Even though she COULD make a lot of money, she was stuck in feast-or- famine mode. She would periodically PACK her schedule with work, bill a METRIC shit ton of money, and then CRASH from exhaustion.

The inevitable crash of exhaustion would cost her work, sometimes whole clients. She'd lose her sanity as balls dropped, clients would fall by the wayside, and she'd despair. The money would dry up and she'd panic.

Her schedule would clear and she'd rest, and then have to start over, only to build back up to the same frantic pace when she recovered.

She spent years stuck in this cycle.

One of her deep fears was that success would cost her her sanity and health – because it WAS costing her that.

So she periodically sabotaged her business just to get some rest.

When we started working together I asked her to build in one day for rest, include a daily lunch break, and choose an hour each day by which to "close shop" for her personal life. It was a huge leap, and I (and my team of coaches) was there to support her through the inner pieces.

One of the ways we re-trained her brain was to see that even with a full schedule of clients, we could build in time for HER through her work day. We began creating saner work schedules together. She advanced to planning in time for her, time for passion projects, creativity, and rest. She grew more picky about whom she took on as clients. She began only working with people she LIKED, and set containers and boundaries around the work she did for them.

There was work around healthy boundaries, expectations of deserving abundance even if she WASN'T killing herself, and being worthy of a joyful work day that didn't run her ragged.

If we had JUST worked on her work hours and "time management," she would have kept sabotaging because her subconscious is STRONG (like yours and mine) and would have kept running the show behind the scenes.

ADDITIONALLY, having some space to breathe and evaluate and work ON her business instead of constantly serving clients allowed her to step back and see that not

ALL her clients were ideal clients.

Over the next year of working together she had the bandwidth to start letting go of non-ideal clients (the ones that made her crazy and took up most of her time) and clarify and ATTRACT her IDEAL clients – the dream clients who allowed her to be working less and making more money – TRIPLING her income and projecting to QUADRUPLE it by the end of the year.

I want to highlight that for both her, and me (back in the day with MY coach) it was the COMBO of the inner work, the digging, the support around what the most effective strategies would be for the goals we wanted, what we were offering, and how we most loved working, combined with where our subconscious had a foot on the brake – THAT'S the combo that brought the big change.

The right planning, support, and accountability is what it will take to move your business to whatever your next level is. It won't happen by accident.

AND---> it won't happen by you doing the same things that AREN'T getting you where you want to be and just PRAYING they'll work. You're going to have to do something different to get a different result.

(Say it with me: "The definition of insanity is doing the same thing over and over and expecting different results.")

The actual results that I saw the year that I planned ahead made a believer out of me.

> That was the turning point, because that year
> I made more money **and I worked less hours.**

Because let's be honest, if the story was that I put in twice the hours and made more money (as a result of giving up my life), *it's just not that appealing. I don't think this is what ANY of us want.*

Once I realized the power of effective planning and utilizing Sacred Structure to learn how to BEND TIME (or create the feeling of expansive time, of free time, of time that worked FOR ME INSTEAD OF me trying to work for time...) for my life, there was no turning back.

That's why I absolutely love helping women like you create a clear path to running a business that's fulfilling, brings in all the income you need, **AND gives you the freedom to enjoy it and do more and more of the work that you love!**

THAT'S THE HOLY GRAIL, right there. :-)

So the tools I'm going to teach you are ones that you can use every quarter, even every week if you want. These tools – and time, itself – bend and stretch to fit YOU, not the other way around.

You can use these tools to plan your day, week, month, quarter, year, personal life AND biz – so they're really widely applicable. You can also use them to plan out shorter projects or areas of focus.

Time On, In, and OFF

Here's where multi-passionate women entrepreneurs get stuck and miserable.

A host of ills comes when your schedule (Sacred Structure) – which is really just about how you spend your time – **doesn't match what's actually most important to you.**

When you're not spending time doing what matters most to you, you may experience any of the following:

- ★ **Burnout**
- ★ **Overwhelm**
- ★ **Disconnect**
- ★ **Depression**
- ★ **Physical illness**
- ★ **Unsatisfying personal relationships**
- ★ **Stress, anxiety, and depression**
- ★ **Exhaustion and lack of energy...**
- ★ **(That's a short list. Feel free to add your own.)**

Ironically, the above can actually make it impossible for you to motivate yourself to do things you love in any remaining free time. It becomes a black hole of energy drain, time suck, and misery.

Often when you're spending your time doing things that aren't meaningful to you, when you DO have free time, you're disconnecting and trying to numb yourself/self-soothe/relax from a day that sucked at your soul.

For instance, many of us spend a CRAZY amount of our non-work time watching TV or scrolling the social media pages, hitting that "thumbs up" or "heart" icon.

I get stuck in this myself.

Mostly during times where I'm overbooking myself, spreading myself thin, taking on other people's energy, or not making time for the cornerstones of my sanity, like time outdoors, my spiritual practice, unscheduled time in my calendar, time with my Kiddo, and sleep, I notice that the slope gets REAL slick, REAL quick. The more overwhelmed and spread thin I get, the more compelling Netflix binges are, or spending HOURS scrolling the F-Book and IG pics.

Every extra hour I'm stuck there makes it HARDER to get up and do something that actually nurtures and feeds me.

No matter what phase or type of business you're in, not having your heart-centered priorities straight can be a kiss of death, in both your professional AND your personal life.

If you're not able to create the time and space to do everything that needs to be done, including all the things you love that feed your heart, mind, and body...**it can literally mean that your biz doesn't thrive or grow. OR, it can mean that it ONLY grows at the expense of your sanity, joy, and well-being.**

I see this time and time again: a business takes off like gangbusters, which feels like a dream come true. I mean, that's the hope, right? Business builds quickly, clients are happy and referring new clients, your product or service

TAKES off, and business is FLOWING. That's what you want, right?

Of course. BUT this can be as deadly as the opposite. I'll show you why.

What often happens in this scenario is one of two things. Sometimes it's BOTH:

1. The business leaps forward, without a structure, systems, standard operating procedures (SOPs) or organization. So the more work, the more business, the more TIME and sanity it costs you. This eventually results in burnout, income at the cost of sanity and happiness, or DEEP sacrifice in the name of your work.

2. The business leaps forward, but because you haven't mastered your time or set up healthy boundaries, it becomes parasitic and feeds off your life energy in order to thrive. It grows and grows, while your energy and joy shrinks and shrinks. You wind up compromising by sacrificing your own time, your own health, your own passions and well-being for the life of your work. No bueno.

Either way, you soon reach a ceiling of hours in the day. Without time management, healthy boundaries, or solid SOPs, it's really hard to bring on a team, delegate, and work smarter rather than harder. It becomes increasingly hard to climb back out.

CASE STUDY: LISA

I had a client who came to me in this exact situation. Lisa hung up a shingle as a service provider, did a good job for her first few months of clients, and was QUICKLY on her way to booking her days solid with new clients.

I warned her right away that her problem wasn't going to be CREATING growth.

It was going to be BALANCING her growth with building a solid infrastructure for her company and then being able to LEVERAGE her time so that her success didn't run her ragged.

In the beginning of her program she worked really hard to start creating standard operating procedures (SOPs) and systems that would help her organize her time. We started to work on how she could find reliable folks to train and install under her, so that she could move to management of her team while they did the day-to-day client work. This was the key to growing her income and capability to serve more and more clients WITHOUT working, herself, every waking hour.

But she got stuck. She wasn't making time for the program, for our work together. She took on more and more clients in a fearful reflexive sort of "feast or famine" panic and ignored creating the infrastructure and doing the work to bring on a team. She booked herself solid.

Predictably she started to burn out. She began making mistakes, her clients became unhappy, and the constant work started to burn her out emotionally and physically.

Then she collapsed, taking her business with her. She had to completely STOP working to regain her health and sanity.

Her business folded because she hadn't successfully trained anyone to work with her. She left a group of unhappy clients behind that she had bailed on in some way, which meant that when she DID go back, she'd have to rebuild instead of just stepping back in.

She ghosted from our program which meant that she lost access to ALL the support that could have helped her put a pause on her business without losing the ground she had earned and having to start over.

And her business failed – with considerable emotional distress and personal disaster in the process.

For a healthy work/life balance AND a thriving business, it's crucial to have time to work not just IN your biz (this can be considered the time you spend DOING the thing you do, with your clients, etc.) but also ON your biz – INCLUDING the time to create the organization and structure I just mentioned.

Then, of course, you need to make sure that EVERY WEEK there's a healthy balance of time OFF: laptop closed, phone on vibrate, and your time spent with family, friends, out-doors, reading, sleeping in, cooking good food, resting, moving your body, etc.

{NOTE: *Without the above, success – no matter how much money is involved – will never FEEL like success.*}

Your time spent ON your biz is where the growth is. (Read that again.)

Your time ON is where you nurture and grow your audi-ence and community, feed your visibility, and increase your expertise and platform as a go-to person in your field.

It's where you build connections and start relationships that you can nurture as people begin to trust you, feel familiar with you, and LIKE you.

Time ON is your planning, marketing, and strategizing time. It's like weeding, watering, and fertilizing your crops instead of just dropping seeds and then leaving them in the field untended.

MANY multi-passionate and witchy women biz own-ers and entrepreneurs totally miss this work on a regular basis **because you're stuck in putting-out-fire mode** and not able to make the time for GROWTH. You're not able to make the time to actually nurture the seeds you planted so they eventually bear fruit for you.

The Heart-Centered Priorities (HCP) practice that's coming up is super important because it teaches you to get clear from the jump about what your top HCP are. Once those are clear and spelled out, they become your guiding light.

ANY *plan for growth* **MUST** *take the results of this practice into serious consideration, yet* **MOST** *entrepreneurs and business owners* **SKIP** *this step and work according to cultural or familial definitions of success that often (with a little reflection)* **AREN'T EVEN YOURS.**

For instance, many of us grew up with a cultural definition of success that includes bigger homes, flashy or new cars, lots of/nicer clothing, and vacations and second or third homes.

I'm sure your family/culture/social circle has common definitions of success and some of those might be shared by you, but some might not be what's actually important to you. **If you're not conscious of what's MOST important to you, you might be building plans that lead you to empty victories.**

Insight Exercise

What were some of your family/cultural/social circle definitions of success?

★ _____

★ _____

★ _____

★ _____

★ _____

CASE STUDY: Thea

A few years ago I worked with a talented woman who was the head of a multi-million dollar company. She hired me to help solve problems within her marketing strategies and messaging that were hurting their bottom line.

She had a BEAUTIFUL home in a gorgeously quaint town. Her clothing and style were impeccable. She had a really nice car that started every time she turned the key. :-) She was able to take vacations, eat at the best restaurants, and had a banging social life.

However, when we had our first consultation, what I ALSO heard was that she felt immensely guilty because her little kid was in aftercare all week until 6 pm because of all the extra time she was putting in at her company.

The pressure that she was under to increase her company's performance caused her to prioritize turning the company around versus spending more time with her kid and on her own happiness.

This caused massive guilt (for her) and stress (for both her and her kid) as she worked around the clock in her business, and her personal life and relationships suffered more and more.

So in our first session together, in addition to her specific business goals, I asked her what she'd like for HER, in HER personal life.

She set the goal to get her kiddo out of aftercare by the time we finished working together.

With her HCP and some tweaks in her strategies and how she spent her day, we got her kid home at 3 pm every day TWO WEEKS INTO WORKING TOGETHER.

We structured her day (AND, of course, part of this was our work around making her strategies more effective so she was actually working SMARTER instead of HARDER) so that she could break at 3 to pick up her kiddo, come home, do another hour of work, and then shut the laptop

(WITHOUT GUILT) for the rest of the evening for family time and time for herself.

Imagine the impact that had on her life, her kid's life, and their relationship? Their mental health. THAT was a marker of success so deeply personal to her and much more important than money or a new car.

Have Some Gold, Girl.

Why is the HCP exercise so effective?

Imagine for a minute that I gave you one precious cup of liquid gold, enough to last you for the rest of your life.

Would you carry it around in your hands, hoping you didn't lose too much as it dripped through your fingers?

Would you put it in a dixie cup or stuff it in a drawer?

I'm betting that you would do NO such thing, and instead would find a strong, water-tight container in which to hold this precious substance – this treasure that you were only getting this one opportunity to have, that, if you took good enough care of, *would last you your whole life.*

Am I right?

Your TIME is liquid gold. *You only get a certain amount of it and when it's gone you can't get more. What you have right now*

CAN be enough to create everything you deeply desire...if you treat it with respect and care, if you value it and use it wisely.

Your Sacred Structure (or schedule) IS the strong, water-tight container that you use to hold and contain, shelter and guard, your precious **time, the gold in this analogy**.

Without the container of Sacred Structure, your time, **and I know you've felt this**, will literally slip through your fingers, away from you.

Your HCP & Worksheet

So what ARE your HCPs? How do you find them?

Let's dive in.

Note: If you'd prefer a streamlined worksheet that I made for you to actually print out and use, just go to the bonus page I've built for you: *https:// InArmsCoaching.com/bookfreegift*

Heart-Centered Priority & Bull's Eye Exercise:

Creating Your Current Bull's Eye

Let your eyes float closed for a minute and think about the ways that you spend your time right now – all the ways that your energy and time get spent these days. And I don't mean ideally, but how they **actually** get spent.

Think about the people in your life, the work, the errands, tasks, responsibilities, trips, commitments...

the things that you spend the MOST amount of time and energy on right now.

And then open your eyes and just begin to jot it all down in front of you in a simple list... so: kids, car, dog, groceries, meals, friends, work, housework, relationships, family commitments, etc....

What I'm Currently Spending My Time & Energy On:

1. _____

2. _____

3. _____

4. _____

5. _____

6. _____

7. _____

8. _____

Draw a bull's eye with three circles around the center (or just go download the worksheet I made for you. https:// InArmsCoaching.com/bookfreegift

In the center ring write the top 1-2 items that you spend the most amount of time and energy on: job, kids, fears, etc. That goes right in the center.

In the second ring pick the 2-3 things that you spend the second most amount of time and energy on.

In the third ring pick the 2-3 things that you spend the third most amount of time and energy on.

Any remaining items get placed along the outer edges.

Look at this bull's eye and think about how it feels to have your daily life prioritized this way. What do you notice? How does it feel to you? What do you wish there were less of? More of?

And, where does your business or work goal for this program come in?

Write down the top 3 emotions that this bull's eye makes you feel.

   ★ How I currently spend my time makes me feel

   _____.

   ★ How I currently spend my time makes me feel

   _____.

   ★ How I currently spend my time makes me feel

   _____.

   ★ What are you seeing here for yourself?

   _____.

Creating Your Ideal Bull's Eye

Begin to think about what you'd **like to consciously be giving energy to**, asking your heart what it wants – what it needs you to be directing time and energy to in the next 3-6 months.

And imagine your life exactly the way you want it to be, full of the things you love, full of activities, people, experiences, places that make you feel good, the work or business that brings you joy.

Imagine filling your day-to-day life with people and situations that FEED you, that GIVE you energy. That make you feel good.

Then open your eyes and start making a list of the top 8 people, experiences, or work that you'd IDEALLY like to be spending the most amount of your time and energy on.

What I'd Ideally LOVE to Be Spending My Time & Energy On:

1. _____

2. _____

3. _____

4. _____

5. _____

6. _____

7. _____

8. _____

Think about where you WANT to focus and direct your energy and time in these next 3-6 months:

What do you want to create, manifest, work towards?

Draw another bull's eye.

Find the one or two items that are most important and write them in the center circle.

Then find the one or two things that are second most important, remember, JUST for the next 3-6 months – and write them in the second circle, and so on.

Now look at your ideal bull's eye, really focusing on how the energy of it feels, how it feels to set the intention to direct your energy towards these priorities and write the first 3 emotions that come to mind.

* When I think about spending my time this way it feels _____.

* When I think about spending my time this way it feels _____.

* When I think about spending my time this way it feels _____.

And notice again where your business/work comes in and how it feels in balance with the rest of your Heart-Centered Priorities.

What are you seeing here for yourself?

* _____
_____
_____
_____
_____
_____
_____
_____

Once you're clear on WHAT'S most important to you and how it compares to how you currently spend your time right now, it's going to be much easier to create a filter for how you spend your time, and on WHAT.

This is REALLY important because for everything that you're spending time on now that isn't REALLY important to you, **you're losing energy**. It's also feeding outdated beliefs and patterns of thinking that are (guaranteed to be) jamming you up in more areas than just your business (like your love life, financial situation, or even your health).

The question is, now what? How on earth do you build a schedule that puts your priorities front and center?

Q: WAIT – CAN I DO THAT? Can I truly organize my time according to what I love MOST?

Yes.

Yes, you can.

In fact, I would argue that to be the magick-maker that you know you are, to do the magick you're called to do, to have all the room for the things you love, you MUST put the things you love FIRST, and learn how to bend your time to your will so that you have SPACE for joy, balance, and peace of mind.

OTHERWISE WHAT'S THE POINT??

This is TOTALLY possible. I've helped HUNDREDS of women create this, and I can help you, too.

HOWEVER, it's really important to note that sustainable change doesn't happen overnight, and in the creation of a

sustainable Sacred Structure for yourself and your work, you're going to need to look at the inner pieces that are connected to why your time doesn't always work for you so far. It's a PRACTICE, not a destination. Suffice to say, there's a lot of this that's about YOU, and for the results you want to change, you're going to have to bravely face the parts of YOU that are invested in NOT CHANGING.

This is one of the many reasons I call this work a *magickal practice*.

You have to start where you stand.

With YOU.

How your time feels won't change until YOU change how you feel about your time, and remove any inner blocks around using time the way you want.

Time AND magick are about energy and focus.

If your time isn't working for you, it's because of YOU – and you'll need to first and foremost OWN that. That work, and the accompanying transformation, isn't a one-time change, or a massive overnight shift that can be made.

This is one of the reasons that my clients work with me in my programs – and often wind up enrolling in program after program for YEARS as they watch their results grow in quantum leaps OVER TIME. This work is not like a New Year's Resolution that you throw yourself into making and then drop 2 weeks later. (Not if you want the incredible ful-filling life that's waiting for you.)

It takes time, inner work, and lots of support to ACTU-ALLY change the way you do things, the way you think about things, and your attachments to both things that work for you AND things that don't.

The beauty of this work is that when you start to make the shifts, your days instantly *feel* better. You're no longer trapped in a never-ending loop of frustration anymore. You know you own your time, *even* if it takes time to implement all of the changes you want to make.

Chapter 4

The Big Rocks

In the last chapter you sat down with the exercises for finding your heart-centered priorities and crafting your current and ideal bull's eye. I strongly suggest you print that out (from the bonus page of goodies I made for you through the Bonus Gift Link) and use it to work through the Bull's Eye exercise. I made it just for you – so go grab it if you haven't already!

Once you're done...what do you do with that piece of work?

How do you start creating a way of structuring your time that allows your heart-centered priorities to actually **be prioritized** in your day-to-day without all the other STUFF getting in the way and derailing what YOU want?

I think in images most of the time. Here's a way I like to imagine this next exercise: What if I gave you three fist-sized rocks, a huge mason jar, and a bunch of tiny pebbles, and asked you to fit them all into that big mason jar?

What would your strategy be?

I can tell you from experience that this will only work if you put the BIG rocks in first, and then let the pebbles fill the spaces around them.

The big rocks symbolize your priorities. They're the ones in your second, IDEAL Bull's Eye. **The pebbles** are everything else that needs your time and attention, including the tasks and pieces that aren't necessarily your heart-centered priorities or even 100% within your control.

Now, before we go any further I want you to think for a minute about how you structure your time, physically. Do you use a daily planner? An online calendar?

What's important to you in terms of how you manage and look at your time? That you are able to handwrite your schedule? That your team members can have access to it to book appointments or serve your clients with their scheduling needs?

When I started In Arms Coaching I used the most beautiful, witchy day planner by a group of women called We'Moon. I loved it. I loved reading it, looking at the pictures, and writing out my appointments in the little blocks of space for each day.

But as IAC grew, my We'Moon planner stopped working for me.

For one thing, it didn't have time slots so I could see my day planned out by the hour. It didn't give much ROOM for each day, so it was hard to get in my shifts at work, client sessions, and personal appointments for myself or the Kid each day. (There was a lot going on then! Well, not that there isn't NOW, but back then there were multiple jobs to juggle, too, and I was doing it all as a single parent...)

When I hired my first team member about a year in who took over scheduling, I couldn't share my We'Moon with her virtually, and we had to move to Google calendars.

Thirteen years later, I have a Google calendar that is shared with my dog rescue coordinators, my IAC team, my husband, and the Kiddo, and can have LOTS of things directly imported into it such as educational classes, podcast interviews, etc. It's a life saver, for real.

What you use isn't as important as the fact that you use something that works for you, so I want you to think about whether or not what you're using IS working for you.

If it is, take it out now. If it's not, now is the time to decide on another scheduling tool that does. You'll need it for the next part.

Examples:
Google calendar
Paper calendar or planner (if you don't need the time slots, I LOVE We'Moon's planners) – desk version, wall version, book, etc.

Your Time Is Your Container

At this point, you've looked at how you spend your time now.

You've looked at how it feels, and what is and isn't getting done. You've been able to create a visible image of how you are currently prioritizing your time, ideal or not.

You've also looked at how you would ideally LIKE to spend your time, how you'd like to prioritize your energy, attention, and work, and how THAT would feel.

You can also see what would change if you were able to structure your time according to what matters the most to you.

CASE STUDY: Amanda

When my client, Amanda, had her 9-to-5 job, her time was not her own. She had two young children and if they were sick she had to hope that she had a sick day to take so she could stay home with them. She had to find them camps, day care, and sitters all summer long. She HATED that. Sometimes when they needed her she DIDN'T have any time off, and she'd lose pay.

So she decided to go out on her own and start her own business.

She began by creating a container for her time that allowed her to put the kids, AND her, first.

Within her first year of business she had structured her time so that her work was 95% finished by the time they got off the bus each afternoon.

She also changed her hours during the summer.

Now, in the summer months she works early mornings with her clients, leaves the middle of the day free and clear for summer activities and sitting by the river with the kids, and then finishes up the odds and ends of her work day after they're asleep, because she LIKES working late at night when the house is quiet and she has had the entire day free.

This is HER version of Sacred Structure. Her happiness comes first and that FEELS like success, even BEFORE she filled her client list and had to start turning away work.

In Amanda's words:

"You helped me see that there really IS a way to structure my time without losing my mind or dropping balls in the process.

I had been taught to think of, and look at, time management and scheduling in a very masculine, linear (and corporate) manner – and that doesn't work well when you are a woman with priorities other than work!

You taught me that my schedule can be fluid and still supportive.

You also provided the ongoing support and the inner work support that I needed to have to release the guilt I felt around not always being business-focused, or not always being mom-focused.

From working with you, I have been able to build a business from my HEART.

One that helps support the LIFE that I am focused on creating and living.

We don't get to leave ANYTHING as women... there's no walking out the door of work and not thinking about it for the rest of the night... there's no leaving parental responsibilities behind when we are in work-mode. We DO IT ALL, all the time.

My work with you, and learning Sacred Structure, created the container I needed to be able to balance doing it all the time :)

I wouldn't be where I am today without you, and it."
Amanda Lopes, Refocus on Being

So how do you turn that list you made in the last chapter into a way of living the hours of your day?

Everything we're doing together in this book will be an important first step, but it's not exactly a silver bullet on its own. Sustainable change is made by setting and implementing small, do-able steps over time, rather than one big, sweeping, dramatic change.

Target Practice

We're going to start with your focal point, or goal.

I ALWAYS want you to start here. Imagine that you and I were planning an exciting road trip together and I asked you to map out the route, making sure we hit towns with independent coffee shops and health food stores every time we stop (because that's something that I would totally do).

Your first question, I imagine, and 100% necessary to find the best routes, would be along the lines of, "Well, where are we GOING, Britt?"

Imagine if I said, "Oh, we'll figure it out. Just plan the route and we'll talk about it later."

It would be REALLY hard to pick the best route, with the stops that we needed, if you weren't clear on where you were GOING, right?

Now, that's a really clear way of seeing how nonsensical it is to try and pick the most effective actions/strategies/plans when you don't have a clear, concise goal or focal point.

Your clear goal determines the best strategies.

First step:

Choose a focal point for this time next year. (Remember the *Sons of Anarchy* story? This is like Tara's target).

{Note: I condensed this exercise to fit here, BUT if you'd like the WHOLE worksheet and prefer a pretty, printable worksheet, just go to the bonus page I've built of resources I want you to have

https://InArmsCoaching.com/bookfreegift}

In your business, what's a goal, focus, or result you'd like to reach by this time next year?

Make it measurable and clear.

Write it down here:

_____

_____

_____

_____

_____

(Example: Instead of "more free time," state clearly "weekends off, guilt free, with no work Saturday or Sunday." Instead of "more money," choose "50K more in revenue by _____.")

In your personal life, what's a goal, focus, or result you'd like to reach by this time next year?

(Again, you want this clear and measurable: Pilates 3 times a week. A date night out of the house once a week. Eight hours of sleep a night. Weekly lunch with a friend, or social hour.)

Write it down here:

_____

_____

_____

_____

_____

_____

Now, are these two focal points already listed in your ideal list and bull's eye, in terms of the work they'll require?

For instance, if your personal goal for the year is to make yoga class 4 times a week, or cook healthy meals from scratch 5 days a week, are YOU and your self-care in your ideal bull's eye?

If enrolling 5 new clients a month is your goal in your business, and you need to build your community to do that, is community growth a priority in your professional focus for the year?

Next step:

You're going to start small by going back to that list you made of how you'd **ideally** like to be spending your time (with anything new that was added from above).

Think of it this way: if there's something you want to harvest this time next year, you're going to need to plan to focus on planting the seeds and nurturing and tending them consistently over the next 9-12 months.

If business growth is a priority for you, there are some strategies that you **absolutely** must be making time for now in your Sacred Structure, like:

→ growing your community (this might include your email list and your social media groups or following)

→ building your network (of potential prospective clients, referral partners or sources, and people who support you and your work and want to hear what you have to say)

→ putting out freebies or ways for people to sample your work (building relationships, trust, and your email list)

→ getting systems in place and making time for working on the bigger picture of your biz...

...that's all considered part of the work ON your biz that we were talking about earlier.

CASE STUDY: Nikki

Nikki had incredible talent and expertise as a 5-time self-published author, and a lifelong writer, educator, and community builder.Yet her professional community for her book-midwifing services (teaching people with stories or areas of expertise how to translate them into a book) was small and insular.

As a result, her brilliantly helpful services and offerings for people who wanted to get their story out into the world weren't selling – even though when they DID, they helped her clients immensely.

She was all over the place trying different strategies to engage her audience and grow it within the communities she was already a part of.

"As a Virgo, I'm generally pretty good at planning and staying organized. Yet often, when I started my book midwife business, I felt like my constantly expanding to-do list was a marathon that I couldn't win. Britt's system of sacred structure has helped me in several significant ways.

Starting with the end goal – the actual top priorities in my life as a whole – was a game-changer. It's much easier to see what things I really DON'T need to do.

Also, when I did my biz planning for the year, I always packed it with WAY too many big projects. Then I'd be super discouraged when I didn't achieve even a fraction of them. Britt has guided me to narrow it down so that my action steps are achievable. This is especially true in the area of community growth, which is one of the broad areas that I've been focused on building. My tendency was to do (or try to do) All The Things – workshops, social media posts, joint venture projects, podcasts, guest blogging, networking... I was running myself ragged, until I got discouraged again and would do nothing.

Over the past couple of years, with Britt's help, I've narrowed it down to just three main things to focus on as I build my community. And guess what? It's working!

Finally, Britt has helped me make regular planning part of my spiritual practice. Each week I sit down with my bullet journal, crystals, and oracle cards for my sacred strategy ritual. It makes the process sacred, and that gives me the incentive to keep doing it, as I love rituals and magick."

Nikki Starcat Shields, book Midwife
and Tranformational Writing Retreat Leader

You also need to be marking out your time IN your biz: appointments with clients, office hours, etc.

AND, of course, you need ample time off (and by OFF I mean laptop closed, phone away, and you being able to check out without guilt, without answering biz phone calls or email).

{SIDE NOTE: **If time management has been a nightmare for you then you might have started this book feeling like any decent time off is an impossibility. THAT'S OKAY. I'm going to show you how to build SLOWLY, without any dramatic, triggering changes that would ultimately just throw you deeper into overwhelm and sabotage.**}

My bull's eye is pretty much always my self-care, my family, In Arms Coaching, Pittie Posse, and my super small circle of women cohorts.

This means that when I'm scheduling my time, I and my family come first, IAC and PP come next, and my cohorts come third.

So an average weekly scheduling session might look like me putting in my own pilates or kickboxing classes, a massage, specific time off, along with anything the kids, my man, or the dogs need. Then comes professional commitments, focus, and projects, and then social engagement.

EVERYTHING else gets fit in around that.

Here's an example of my weekly set-up.

You can see it, but I color code: light blue for personal, dark blue for IAC, and orange for Pittie Posse.

Example Weekly Schedule

Time	Monday	Tuesday	Wednesday	Thursday	Friday	Saturday	Sunday
6:00 AM							
6:30 AM							
7:00 AM	Meditation, stretching: 7-8am	Meditation, stretching: 7-8am	Meditation, stretching: 7-8am	Meditation, stretching: 7-8am	Meditation, stretching: 7-8am		
7:30 AM							
8:00 AM	Monday Rooting: writing, emails, getting into my week: 8-10am	Writing: 8-10am	BNI Rising Tide: 8:15-9:45am	Writing: 8-9:30am	Writing, tying up loose ends: 8-10:30am		
8:30 AM							
9:00 AM							
9:30 AM				PP work: 9:30am-12:30pm			
10:00 AM	Client calls: 10am-12pm	Time on FB groups: 10-11am	BNI 1:1 meetings: 10-11am				
10:30 AM							
11:00 AM		Blog post and social media 11am-12pm	Lunch break: 11am-12pm		My time: lunch with friends, long walks... 11am-1pm		
11:30 AM							
12:00 PM	Lunch break: 12-1:30pm	Group calls: 12-2pm	Client calls: 12-3:30pm				
12:30 PM				Lunch break: 12:30-1:30pm			
1:00 PM							
1:30 PM	Client calls: 1:30-3:30pm			PP work: 1:30pm-4:30pm	Pilates: 1:30-2:30pm		
2:00 PM							
2:30 PM							
3:00 PM							
3:30 PM							
4:00 PM							
4:30 PM	Kickboxing: 4:45pm		Kickboxing: 4:45pm				
5:00 PM							
5:30 PM							

Take a moment now to imagine what YOUR ideal schedule could look like:

Blank Weekly Schedule

	Monday	Tuesday	Wednesday	Thursday	Friday	Saturday	Sunday
6:00 AM							
6:30 AM							
7:00 AM							
7:30 AM							
8:00 AM							
8:30 AM							
9:00 AM							
9:30 AM							
10:00 AM							
10:30 AM							
11:00 AM							
11:30 AM							
12:00 PM							
12:30 PM							
1:00 PM							
1:30 PM							
2:00 PM							
2:30 PM							
3:00 PM							
3:30 PM							
4:00 PM							
4:30 PM							
5:00 PM							
5:30 PM							

It's a radical idea to imagine your ideal schedule, isn't it? That's always sad to me – that it's so hard to imagine being FULLY in control of our own time and how we spend it. How on earth did we get here? (See Patriarchy rant in Chapter One)

The point is that it's time to stop letting the momentum of endless demands whip us around like frayed flags in the wind and start CREATING the lives we want!

For my own sanity I like lots of blocks of unstructured time. Generally, after 3:30 pm every day is family stuff: dinner making, kickboxing class with the Kid, dog walking, chicken care, house stuff (yes, you read that correctly, it says, "chicken care." I have 9 fluffy, silly chickens that I adore.).

We eat like old people (between 5-6 pm usually), and that allows me lots of time in the evening. Right now that's filled with hours of reading for my magickal studies, couples-connecting work with Sully, time with the Kid, conversations, baking, baths and whiskey, and sometimes a Netflix binge.

Weekends are family stuff, home care, self-care, and usually lots of Pittie Posse work or events, because that's what I LOVE doing in my free time.

Having clarity around your ideal schedule is important, additionally, because it allows you to easily pour new requests or potential distractions through the filter of your bull's eye priorities **to see if the new item you're considering adding supports your priorities or not.**

I'll be speaking more to that later when we talk about guidelines for making Sacred Structure work for you.

Getting Started

Okay, are you ready for the next step?

Go back to your Bull's Eye exercise and look at the goals you just wrote out for each area: self and work.

For each goal, think about the 6-7 actions that need to be taken to achieve them.

For instance, say your biz goal is to fill a new program by this time next year.

Some of the actions that need to be taken to achieve that would include:

→ Growing your community so you have more new people to invite in (this is a huge part of what I teach women to do in my programs). This could include focusing on goals around your newsletter, social media engagement, any promotional events, classes you're offering, etc.

→ Getting all the back end pieces of the program ready: content, enrollment process and systems, payment systems, admin, creating materials.

→ Creating a marketing and launch campaign, with all THOSE moving pieces.

→ Building an editorial calendar to educate your existing community about what you're doing and why they need it.

...to name just a few things. :-)

NOW, if the above were your goal, you would begin by creating time each week (or on a monthly basis, depending on what works for you) that you could just call "program creation" or something like that.

The idea is that if you want a full program in a year, you're going to need time and focus to make that happen. **SO you create a block in your calendar just to work on that.**

If you're starting work on it immediately, the time you have available to devote to it might be less than you ideally, eventually want. THAT'S OKAY. It's because you're putting something into a calendar that's already probably quite full.

It's okay to start small.

I repeat: It's okay to start small.

Right now, schedule it in for 15 minutes a week. 30 minutes next month. An hour or two the next month. Soon you'll get to a page in your calendar where you're not already booked, and you can block out the ideal amount of time that you want to spend.

EXAMPLE: *I decided to bite the bullet and start Pittie Posse Rescue in the fall. At that point I could only schedule an hour or two a week for it because I was working with a full calendar. But by the end of the year I had cleared a full day for it once a week. By January (again, it was early fall when I was blocking this all out), I had way more unscheduled time in my calendar, so I started blocking out one full day a week for it – sometimes more.*

Sometimes when I'm working hard on a goal, I'll create time each week for it (I have time each week set aside for social media content batching, being in my group member areas, and networking) but often I'll also create larger blocks of time.

For instance, every other week we schedule a week OFF of being IN my biz (in other words, a client-free week) to JUST focus ON my biz.

That's often where I'll create content, do larger marketing work, or work a whole lot on a book (like this one!) or course.

What would you do with a week off just to work ON your biz?

★ _____

★ _____

★ _____

★ _____

★ _____

★ _____

I do the same thing with Pittie Posse. Every few months I take a whole week JUST for Pittie Posse, and that's where I'll work on bigger projects, or get a whole bunch of something done at once.

{What passion project would YOU pursue if (and by *if*, I mean *when*) you had the time? Seriously, when's the last time you even allowed yourself to consider the possibility that you could have a life structure that allowed you to make time for things simply because you're passionate about them?}

Write down a few areas of interest here:

★ _____

★ _____

★ _____

★ _____

★ _____

★ _____

Ok, back to the Bull's Eye exercise. Now that you've taken each goal and written out the larger actions that need to be done for each...

Next, estimate how much time you would IDEALLY like for each goal, on a weekly basis.

For instance, if your personal goal were to learn a new skill, get in shape, and cook healthy meals 5 days a week, you might be adding in a class or two a week. Time in your day to cook. Time for a long walk.

{Side note: **HURRAY** *for you!* *Making personal goals and starting to carve out time for yourself. As it should be, woman – you can't serve anyone from an empty cup!*}

Start with how much time you'd IDEALLY like for these actions, then look in your calendar for time when you aren't booked yet and start to block those spaces off.

For instance, if you'd ideally like to be taking 3 weight-lifting classes a week but there's no WAY that would fit right now, look 3 months out. Would it fit then? Six months out?

BLOCK it out at the first possible time in the future where there's space for it in your schedule.

Get ahead of the avalanche of things that will fill your time, if you let them, and MAKE the space.

Now, let's go back to present day and where you are now: is ONE class possible now? Where might that go?

If you can't even fit one full class right now, would 15 minutes a day, 3x a week fit?

Then maybe next month you could add one class a week.

Start where you are and build up to where you WANT to be.

This is absolutely CRUCIAL. Without doing it this way you set yourself up for failure. Large, sweeping changes are part of black and white thinking and are very difficult to sustain. PLUS, they cause stretching to a point that can be dangerous and cause harm, which will make you have to give up completely or sabotage.

(NOTE: This can be **literally** harmful. For instance, if you go from not working out at all to 3 kickboxing classes a week, you can HURT yourself physically. Not that I know ANY-THING about that, I'm just giving you an example. I would never do anything that self-sabotaging. Just kidding. I actually did it when I started kickboxing classes and I'm working hard on my all-or-nothing tendencies.)

The most effective way to create SUSTAINABLE change that doesn't throw your damned BACK out is to start small and BUILD according to your ability.

M'kay?

From here, break each action into JUST the first 3-4 small steps. A useful guideline is that the small steps should be about 15-to-20-minute tasks.

For instance:

Goal: 20 new clients by _____

Action 1: Grow newsletter
Steps: decide on monthly template, brainstorm 5 topics to write about, poll group about interests

Action 2: 1 webinar a month
Steps: choose 5 topics, pick 5 groups I can promote in, find 10 people who will share and invite people

Action 3: Streamline enrollment system
Steps: write out the journey from prospect to client, list all paperwork, templates/emails necessary, go through old emails to see what already exists to template

Action 4: Get finances in order
Steps: create financial abundance tracking sheet, pick accounting tool, put 10 minutes in each day to check in with my accounts/track finances

Guidelines for Making Sacred Structure Work for You

There are a few guidelines that I've created to help you use Sacred Structure as a living, breathing, evolving tool. These suggestions will also serve to stop you from **seizing up in perfectionism and throwing the whole thing out the window in the first month.**

These guidelines are one of the MOST important pieces of Sacred Structure. Because if you're anything like the incredible driven women I work with, your M.O. is PROBABLY to try and make big changes, get stuck, have it not work perfectly, get overwhelmed and frustrated and BURN THE WHOLE DAMNED THING DOWN.

How's that working out for you?

If it hasn't worked so well for you in the past, keep reading (and applying the steps) and let's set this up differently so that this time, you get different results.

Guideline #1: Anything that goes into the schedule must reflect what you put in your bull's eye image.

This means that when you're asked to commit to something, tempted to take on a new project, or asked for a favor or project involvement, you STOP.

For instance, what if a fellow mom asked you to get involved with a school committee? Or a colleague asked you to join a project she was starting?

{Life-changing tool ahead alert: The Time-Guarding Tool}

---\>I recommend that you NEVER answer requests or offers in the moment, ESPECIALLY if you have people-pleasing tendencies or have trouble saying no, tend to overcommit, or worry about "letting people down."---\<

It's too much pressure, and dammit, you LIKE making people happy, so your go-to answer is going to be a knee-jerk affirmative because it will make them HAPPY, it will be accommodating, it will encourage them to like you more, etc. All the reasons you could say YES when you mean MAYBE or NO.

NOTE: *one phrase I'm living by these days? "NO is a full sentence." Stick that one in your pocket for later.*

Solution: Simply say your own version of, "That sounds interesting. Thanks for asking! **Let me look at my schedule and get back to you.**" (*Those are magic words there, like Jack's beans. Carry them with you, plant them when you can, and you know what you'll grow? MORE TIME. Time devoted to YOUR goals! Imagine what a life you will create that way.*)

Then take the request home with you to feel into, gauge your time, priorities, and what's already on your plate.

See what we did there?

A. **You don't have to risk overcommitting** by answering "yes" in the moment to be agreeable or accommodating.

B. **You don't have to worry about discomfort** if it's more likely that the answer would be a more intuitive "no" to their face.

C. **You don't have to try to figure ANY of this out in the moment** in front of them, or without having space and silence to intuit what works best for you right now.

Instead you can go home and look at your schedule and commitments when you're alone and see if that request or offer feeds any of your top priorities right now.

If the answer is Yes:

Sweet!

AND...DO you have TIME for it right now?

Will it cause you to have to give up or compromise anything else?

Will it cause you stress?

Can you easily fit this in?

Are there any modifications or boundaries that would have to be set ("Yes, I CAN do this, but I need you to know I'll only be able to be available _____ and _____ instead of _____...").

If the answer is No:

Get back in touch and say something like, "Thanks so much for thinking of me. I don't have the bandwidth to devote to this right now, but (please ask me again next year/have you thought of _____, who might be able to...)" etc.

Stop for a second – what would change for you if you were able to consistently and effectively use the above tool? How much time, space, and sanity would it create for you?

Going back to your bull's eye and the big rocks that you made space for in your Sacred Structure, the ones that go into your week first:

What if something comes up that needs to be done but you don't have the bandwidth, or it will take the place of something else that's also important?

Here are some options:

★ **Decide** if it really needs to be done and when (can it wait a few weeks or months?)

For instance, there's an organization that I'm a part of that asked me last year to be on the mentor team to support new members.

I was very excited about that opportunity and dedicating a lot of time to it.

However, I recently got a vision for this tool that I teach clients ALL THE TIME and wanted to make all the content I have for it into a book so more women can find it. (Guess what? I DID IT. It's in your hands RIGHT NOW!)

But I had to make time in an already-packed week to write, almost daily.

Initially, that felt impossible. I'm already running a business, a non-profit, two teams, a household filled with hormonal teen girls, bickering pit bulls, and 9 chickens who won't lay any eggs, I'm enrolled in a super-intensive magickal program, AND taking REALLY good care of myself... WHERE would time to WRITE A BOOK fit in?

Having my time-bending tools IS the reason this not only happened but happened FAIRLY easily without dropping any balls OR "sacrificing" anything else that was important to me.

Here's how I did it:

I looked at the long-term tasks I was working towards every week in my schedule: the mentorship role for the organization, the work I'm doing on Pittie Posse Rescue's infrastructure, and the empty space I have for personal time, and I re-evaluated them all.

Of those commitments the mentorship role felt negotiable to me and easily put on the back-burner, so I reached out and told them I was stepping away for a few months. That freed up at least 2-4 hours a week.

Writing this book moved into that space, and I borrowed a little time additionally from other areas of focus.

It didn't take up any space that would make any of those areas suffer. I just worked with about 5 hours of writing time a week (with a little more on weekends) because it's a finite period of time, AND I know that this book will contribute to the ways I'm able to support women within In Arms Coaching, which IS one of my big rocks.

Additionally, it worked because almost every day what I WANT to do is get up and write. It's a joy-filled, exciting activity to me, so I'm drawn to spending time on it. It's a calling, and callings always feel good to spend time on.

This is ALSO possible because I'm delegating some of the work to a few super-skilled experts: Nikki Starcat Shields, who is a book midwife, who performed content editing of the rough draft and got it to flow better once I finished it, and additionally I have a beloved copywriter who polished my stream-of-consciousness and made it even MORE helpful to you :-).

Then I have an amazingly expert launch strategist who took the finished copy, turned it into a REAL book, and helped me to catapult it out into the world for you to find.

Next option when something comes up that needs to be done but you don't have the bandwidth, or it will take the place of something that's also important:

* ★ **Delegate** it (give it to someone else to hold or execute for you!)

The ONLY reason I've been able to start, grow, and scale a 6-figure business, take deep care of myself, start and grow a pit bull rescue to mainstream recognition, write and publish a book, plan a THIRD business AND have enough free time left over for my sanity **is because I am profoundly expert at DELEGATING and leading my teams.**

Here's the thing: no matter how BAD-ASS you are, you CANNOT DIY THIS (That's Do-It-Yourself, if you're not a crafty witch – it's a term from the craft-home improvement world). No woman is an island. No "successful," happy, healthy woman achieved ANYTHING all by herself. Success takes teamwork, support, delegation, and leadership. **It just does.** No barrier or block you might carry towards any of those things is going to change this fact.

Here are some inner pitfalls you may encounter when trying to master delegation: beliefs that no one will do it as well as you will, reluctance to hand your "baby" over to someone else, a belief that you don't "deserve" to have support, fear that you don't know how to "manage" people, discomfort with leadership...

The above is a SHORT list of fears and limiting beliefs that I (and my team) support women with in my Biz Elementals program ALL THE TIME.

Without seeing these clearly and working through them, you will sabotage any help you can set up.

The third option you have when something comes up that needs to be done when you don't have the bandwidth for it, or it will take the place of something else that's also important:

★ **Do** it after your big rocks are blocked in (once you know what HAS to get time in your schedule, you know if you have wiggle room around those big rocks, and how much).

Guideline #2: For the woman with so many ideas, you can barely focus.

I had had the idea to write a book for a LONG time. In fact, I have two more half-finished books waiting for my attention...but I also get LOTS of other ideas and had to learn how to evaluate them and decide which were going to be seeded now, which might be seeded later, and which just had to be noted and waited on.

Generally women in my community are visionaries and entrepreneurial- minded luminaries. **If that's you, you get new ideas like some people change socks.** Your collective "crow syndrome" (you love and chase bright, shiny objects) can keep you eternally in the "seed" phase, and perpetually challenged to nurture and tend the seeds you planted to the point where you get to enjoy the harvest.

Solution: keep an Idea Journal.

Write all those juicy ideas down in one place to get them out of your head. Then towards the end of the year, take it out and create your SS again for the next year, and decide what's important to add in as a focal point for that year. Then thumb through your Idea Journal and see what will feed and contribute to your big priorities for the next year.

Guideline #3: You can move anything you want around in your schedule, but *don't delete any of the big rocks.*

This means your priorities remain your priorities, and you stay focused (or notice when you get UNFOCUSED and pull your attention back).

For example, my big rocks are my family, In Arms Coaching/Pittie Posse, and self-care.

One Tuesday morning I had an exercise class planned for my self-care. But the sun was out and I wanted to enjoy it with the Kid, who was home.

I thought about my bull's eye and decided I'd go play in the sun with my kid because this still felt like self-care. I then moved my exercise class to the next morning – so it still remained a priority and there was room for both.

IT CAN ALL FIT. (Say that out loud with me.)

{TIP: Because I value flexibility and a certain degree of room for spontaneity, I leave what one of my past clients, Chase Young of The Mommy Rebellion, calls GRACE TIME (also known as wiggle room, or padding). This means that I leave blocks of time in my schedule as open space JUST to be able to move things around. It's always helpful for the last-minute things that get thrown in, or something new I want to focus on, or extra down time.

Remember this childhood game? You have to move the numbers to get them in order. IT ONLY WORKS BECAUSE THERE'S AN EMPTY SPOT. I visualize my calendar like this.

As long as there are some blank spots, I have flexibility to move things around in it.}

Guideline # 4: Every week you get to start over and leave the week before behind.

YAY!

Here's what this means, rockstar: you don't get to tell yourself stories about how you suck when you didn't do everything perfectly the week before. You start over.

WHAT? No self-flagellation? No kicking your own ass? No throwing your arms up in the air? No tantrum at your lack of perfection? No just-letting-the -whole-damned-thing-go because you didn't do it perfectly right out the gate?

Nope. I'm asking you to recognize that that's actually a PERFECT way to sabotage yourself in order to NOT look at what you actually LOVE about NOT having the time and success that you SAY you want.

(This is some of that all-important INNER work that I do with my clients. It's critical to identify the places where you have what I referred to earlier as 'divided will.')

SO, let's get real here: How many times has your attach-ment to doing something "right" or "perfectly" caused you to sabotage and turn completely away from something that actually could have REALLY been helpful, if you had stuck with it?

Here's what you can do now instead when you've "messed up."

At the end of the week:

* **Take a deep breath. This is about PRACTICE, not perfection. You get to start over.**
* **Sit with your priorities for the next week.**
* **Look at your schedule.**
* **Write what you're grateful for and what worked well last week.**
* **Then write down what you'll do differently next week.**

Here's an example. Recently I realized I was flaking on things that were important to me in my schedule. When I reflected on it I realized I felt disconnected to the commitments I had made and the things I put in my schedule. I was unsure that I could stick to it all.

So the following week, KNOWING what hadn't worked the past week, I created a small morning grounding routine to simply connect with what I wanted to do that day and get excited about it. (WAY *better than just delivering a self-inflicted ass-kicking and shaming session.*) *I kept pulse-taking, tweaking, and adjusting until I was getting the things done that I said I wanted to.*

NOTE: *if you keep putting something in your schedule and it KEEPS not happening, it's also important to be honest with yourself about whether or not this is something that you ACTU-ALLY WANT and are excited about committing to. Ask yourself:*

Why do you want it?

What would it mean for you to be successful doing this

thing?

How does it feed your priorities?

OR: If it's not happening, is it something you think you're supposed to want?

Or someone ELSE wants you to want?

What's YOUR motivation for it?

Bonus exercise for Guideline #1:

If you're wondering how to reflect your bull's eye image in an already full schedule, give this a go. We touched on this earlier, but I'll walk you through it for your priorities specifically.

Pick one week. You could start with next week or the first week of next month. Now just put your 3-4 big rocks in first.

My big rocks are:

1. _____

2. _____

3. _____

4. _____

Because you're probably not starting with a blank schedule, you'll need to start by putting in small amounts of time for each of the big rocks and building them up as the weeks go by.

Then, as you reach a time in your calendar where you're not already scheduled (a month out? next quarter?), you can add longer blocks of time for your big rocks until those are able to go in first, before everything else.

Capiche?

The key to making this work for yourself is: slow and steady. **You're obviously not starting with a blank schedule.** Your life isn't beginning next week. You already HAVE a full schedule and a life in progress!

The trick is to work in these little blocks of time over the next few weeks, even if it feels imperfect, even if you're starting with 10- or 15-minute time blocks, until you can shift your schedule into what you REALLY want it to look like.

In fact, write out what an ideal week would look like so you have a picture to aim for.

Note things like:

* ★ Time JUST for you
* ★ Time for sleeping/rest
* ★ Screen-free time
* ★ Time for romance or time with a partner (or time to LOOK for a partner!)
* ★ Quality time with family
* ★ Ideal hours IN and ON your biz. For instance, I like to write early in the day, so I moved my client call hours to start LATER in the morning so that I can write for a few hours first if I choose, even on days that are client-focused. It feels great starting the day by doing one of the things I love most

Write it out. An ideal week for you would include time for:

★ _____

★ _____

★ _____

★ _____

★ _____

While you get in the habit of making time for your WHOLE life, actually block in time for these things.

Consider: Ideally, how many hours would you be working in total each week? What passion projects would you want time for?

Ideally, I'd like to be working _____ hours a week.

I'd like time for the following passion projects:

_____

_____

_____

_____

_____

→ Create an ideal schedule for yourself and put it up on a wall where you can see it every day for inspiration and intention-setting. *Even if it takes you a YEAR to get to this ideal schedule, it's important to have it where you can see it and consider it on a daily basis.*

I'd also like you to notice the perspective switch required to move to owning your time.

For many, many people, your time feels decided FOR you. We learn this as little kids, being forced out of bed in the morning. Most of us were made to go to school, maybe even made to do things AFTER school. Most of us were conditioned to believe that your schedule is something that happens TO you. (Read that again.) Your time is spent on obligations. Even if you've mostly reconciled that as an adult, I bet there are still vestiges of fears, beliefs, and discomfort around the idea of completely owning your time that are lurking in your brain. Even *planning* to have sovereignty over your time is a HUGE energetic shift for many people.

Most of us grow up knowing we HAVE to spend the majority of our time in school. Or learning. We may want to sleep, climb trees, spend hours in imaginative play, paint, dance, or catch frogs.

Many kids have their time tightly scheduled from waking to sleeping. There's an epidemic of children having less and less free, unstructured time.

No wonder as adults we have a terrible time making space for sheer joy, for following our intuitive sense about what feels best, for choosing our own path and deciding when we want to do things and what works for US.

CASE STUDY: Amanda

Some pages ago I mentioned a past client, Amanda. She LIVES for the summer. She LOVES the sun. She LOVES the river she lives by.

When she worked her 9-to-5 job, she lost all her summer days with her kids except her short vacation every year, and she HATED it.

Now, from June through the beginning of September, she arranges her hours the way SHE wants to.

Her workload gets lighter.

She takes a lot of time OFF.

AND, even during the week she often works early in the morning, takes the middle of the day off to be outside with her kids or at the river beach, and then puts in another solid hour or two at night after the kids go to bed.

She LOVES her summer schedule. It works for her.

So far you've gained a new time management tool (based on an approach that reprioritizes the things that matter most to you), a new way to think about your time, and a little bit of perspective on why most time management tools HAVEN'T worked for you yet.

But if I were to leave you here you'd be getting little more than some spoon-fed content that you're supposed to mold yourself into.

We don't play like that. I don't expect you to fit into a box, you unique creature, you.

This is where the magick comes in.

We're going to take this further, and make.it.magickal: energy changing. Perspective switching. Mind-altering.

The REAL meat, the deep, life-changing lessons about why time management has escaped you so far, is yet to come:

Coming up next.... When Sacred Structure DOESN'T Work.

Chapter 5

When Sacred Structure DOESN'T Work.

You've now had a few chapters to work on setting up Sacred Structure – the key tool to understanding how to begin the magick of bending time.

I've said this before, but I'll keep saying it: In order to change the results you've been experiencing up until you started this work, you have to make changes to the way you're currently doing things.

That's a REALLY key piece of making your time work for you instead of the other way around.

If at this point your time still isn't working for you (and you're not feeling satisfying movement using the tools in the past chapters), *you can be sure that there are existing fears, beliefs, and patterns of thinking that are deeply embedded in your system, making it difficult to prioritize your time according to your own needs and desires and allowing you to make sustainable change in how you focus your energy.*

So, once you set up your Sacred Structure you're ready for the next step: **using it to flush out where the thought** patterns that aren't working for you lie. This is where your edge is – and the edge is where the growth happens. It's ALSO the place where you might hit a wall around what you can do for yourself, and what you need some hand-holding, structure, and accountability with. If that's you, I feel you (because that's ME, too)... stay tuned for more on that at the end of this book.

{NOTE: It could take a few weeks of implementing Sacred Structure to see where you're getting in your own way. This is totally normal. The more you track your time – the way you want to use it, and the way you **actually** use it – the more opportunity you'll have to see what part of your brain is ACTUALLY calling the shots.}

Let's look at some of the most common walls that the women I work with initially run into while implementing this tool.

Wall #1: You find yourself attempting to make space for something that has priority for you and then replacing it with something that's "more important." This other thing could be something for someone else, or something you feel guilt over, like a work task that gets prioritized over a personal task.

Here are some things to consider when this happens for you.

Is there a priority that you didn't figure into your bull's eye that keeps popping up?

For instance, say you keep trying to make time to do a yoga video in the middle of the day, but every time you lie on your mat your dog goes crazy and destroys something in the house. You might realize that you didn't schedule time to walk the dog so he isn't crazy. He might not be in your schedule already. You haven't factored in his care as a priority, so it eats (pun intended :-) into the time you've set aside for you.

Or, every weekend day that you plan to relax with a book/ go for a run/take a class/see a friend, a family member asks you to come help with a special project at their house. If you didn't know they had a lot of work on their list that they needed your help with that weekend, you might not have put them into your schedule.

SOLUTION: be honest – one of two things are happening here.

Either there's something that you missed putting into your bull's eye (time to help family, exercise the dog, etc.), OR there are boundaries that need to be asserted. For example, "Hey, Mom, I'd LOVE to help you build that shed. This morning is already committed, but I'd be happy to come over later today to help. I can be there around 3."

{NOTE: setting and maintaining boundaries can be TOUGH. I know that. But they're an essential pillar of Bending Time and creating a life that works for you. It can be uncomfortable to set firm boundaries, especially for people you love. Sometimes the people you love aren't used to you setting boundaries and they rebel a little until they get used to it and grow to expect it.

I work closely with the women in my programs as they learn how to comfortably stand firm and protect their boundaries.

That requires that they take a look at the feelings and beliefs that come up when boundaries are pushed. They might be ready to be transmuted into feelings and beliefs that work BETTER for them (and you, when you do this work!)}

QUESTIONS for you if your "things" just keep getting pushed out of your schedule or disregarded:

1. What do you absolutely LOVE about not doing the thing that you say is a priority? (The concept here is that if you're feeding or continuing to do something, then it's working for you in some way.)

For instance, if I keep putting "read a book" in my schedule, and it's still not happening, there's an attachment to being "too busy to read," or to slowing down, or stopping moving, or not "being productive" that needs to be addressed. Otherwise you can put it in your schedule until the cows come home (*What is THAT saying about? Is it really hard to get cows to come home? It can't be THAT hard*) and it won't happen because some part of you is INVESTED in it not happening.

2. Are there any new boundaries that need to be built, or old ones that need to be reinforced or re-introduced? What would those look like?

WALL #2: There is too much shit on your plate, woman, and it's beyond a DIY situation at this point.

What you might be seeing at this point is that with the priorities you have, you're not actually going to be able to do it alone (*this is a point that EVERY SINGLE ONE of us reaches, and it's actually a sign of success – there's a level of growth happening that means that you need more people to hold it!).* You need more help, a different or new kind of support, or to delegate some of the pieces of what's on your plate. That work is coming. :-)

If I had a quarter for every damned issue we, as the healers, witches, mamas, daughters, and women that we are, carry about GETTING HELP, well, I'd be REALLY, REALLY wealthy.

{I'd have SO many quarters that I'd turn this book into a LUXURY retreat for you all that would be free to attend. It would include daily massages, world-renowned chefs feeding you, and 1 million thread count sheets on your incredible beds. Oh, and pilates classes, a spa... anyway...}

It's REALLY important to understand what your baggage is around receiving, accepting help, asking for help, trusting other people to hold your precious work, being in leadership, managing and guiding people, and asking for what you need...among a few other things.

This book alone isn't going to teach you to do all that (but I sure can, so stay tuned), *but I will say that you will go LITERALLY no further if the above is being carried along with you.* This is one of the areas we provide a LOT of support around in my program, Biz Elementals, because **it is absolutely a do or die issue for your business.** Growth in your business becomes a dead-end if you can't move forward from this point.

BUT you can start here: by being aware of it and seeing what feathers are ruffled as you move forward.

If you're hitting a wall at this point, I'm pretty sure that at least one of those two areas above will resonate for you.

The Value of Sacred Structure NOT Working for You

What I want you to see here is that even when Sacred Structure doesn't work at first, it's REALLY valuable for you. I'll go so far as to say that it's AS valuable for you if it's NOT working (and you stick with it) as it is when it IS working right out of the gate.

Here's why: Every new level of goals that you want to reach is going to require that YOU grow.

→ That you evolve

→ That you get to the edge of your comfort zone and then push yourself a little further

→ That you learn more about yourself

→ That you repattern ways of thinking, and are honest with yourself about your blocks, fears, and beliefs

--->Sustainable growth can't happen without the above. ---<

Changing the Inner Landscape

One of the premises of alchemy and magick is that to exert any change in the outer world, you have to start with where you stand: with yourself.

You have to change the inner landscape before you can change the outer. You have to change YOU before you can change the results you're getting.

And this is hard work.

This is NOT work that the majority of humans commit to.

Nor is it work to be done in isolation.

It's one of the prevailing reasons that there are so many stuck, unhappy people right now.

I can't emphasize this enough. The path that you have dipped a toe into in this book is statistically an infrequently traveled path. The work we're talking about here isn't the fun, glittery work of crystals and burning sage, or affirmations. It's the deeper landscape where the true gold lies.

It's the DEEP, dark, loamy soil inside your psyche. It's about looking at the shameful, hidden, denied, unseen, and repressed parts of yourself, bringing them into the light, being honest and loving with them, and incorporating them into your light. Radically loving and accepting them so you can step fully into the blinding light of your true brilliance.

This work can often be uncomfortable, which is one of the reasons why most people avoid it. But without it you stay put, frustrated, and stunted. The discomfort of moving through it is temporary, the glorious effects of it are ongoing.

It's easier to avoid the deep work, point the finger at others, chant affirmations, and just trudge on the familiar and worn path, even if we're not feeling happy and fulfilled. As a society, it's a cultural norm to numb ourselves instead of looking honestly at our own behavior, motivation, and fears.

We look for pills and insta-remedies to make changes that should start with inner work. Self-examination. Getting to know and understand ourselves better. Radical honesty and acceptance.

{*Side note: this is one reason women go back again and again to the flashy sales pages featuring an e-course, a set of down-loadables, or video content that promises easy overnight change. We really WANT it to be that easy. Just a simple case of some missing info, right? But oftentimes it's pieces within you that are REALLY blocking you, not a lack of information. That's why mentorship and personalized hand-holding is SO crucial to many women's journeys and achievements.*}

The Real Magick

The work that I'm asking you to do in this book is radical and revolutionary in today's culture.

This next part is where the real magick is: the magick of changing the way you think, and where your focus and energy go. Like horseback riding where your "eyes" (or attention) go, is where the horse (or energy) that you're riding will go.

We've been taught, encouraged, even manipulated to NOT know how to REALLY focus our energy.

Because it makes us less powerful. It keeps us spinning. **As we talked about earlier, we live in a world that wants its witches, healers, and powerful women DISTRACTED.**

The toxic patriarchal order that IS, actually relies on us being distracted, exhausted, torn and compromised, and

therefore ultimately WAY less powerful than we COULD be, if only we knew how to get out of our own way and master our time, energy, and focus.

This book, in addition to being about mastering your TIME and filling your schedule according to what you LOVE, *is about the RECLAIMING of your attention, focus, and energy.*

So you can point that bitch where you want and BLAST forward to your heart-centered goals, living on your own terms, and cultivating your version of freedom.

But first, you have to find the stuck parts, the fears, and the old beliefs.

Seeing them clearly and understanding them is the first step. When I work with women in my group programs we do a lot of work around finding, accepting, and releasing these beliefs so that they're not as charged or active and your behavior isn't based on and directed by them.

I like to say that the fears can still ride in the car, but they have to stay in the back seat. They don't get to drive, choose the destination, OR pick the radio station – NO choosing the tunes!

This is so important. Without being really conscious about your old beliefs, patterns of thinking, and fears, you are spending a TREMENDOUS amount of energy and time trying to move forward while you have one foot firmly pressed down on the brake pedal.

What IF Sacred Structure Isn't Working Right Away for Me?

If Sacred Structure works for you right out of the gate, that's amazing. It's important to remember that building a Sacred Structure that works for you is a gradual process that is ALWAYS developing – it's never actually "finished."

Seasonally, I tweak my Sacred Structure. For instance, 6 months ago when I knew this book needed to come forth, I switched my schedule up to make time to write every week.

When I committed to a Carolyn Elliot course, WEALTH, (which, by the way, I HIGHLY RECOMMEND), I made space to have time to read, study, listen to all the calls, and dive deeper into my own magickal practice. As I mentioned before, I shifted everything around again to make space to get this book into your hands.

In the summer I shorten my work days and lighten my schedule to have more time for family and summer fun, because in Maine in the summer we basically all abandon indoor living and spend as MUCH time outside as we can for those two months of good weather. :-)

In the fall, I expand my hours a little and refocus on end-of-year goals, and my focus for the upcoming new year.

I build in spaces that I find I need: like a week JUST for "time on" my biz – without clients – every 5 or 6 weeks. I make sure I have a week OFF every 6 or so weeks. Sometimes I do a Pittie Posse week, where I ONLY focus on Pittie Posse work.

This is easy for me because I've been mastering Bending Time and Sacred Structure for over 15 years. But many women will tell me that they're having trouble making their Sacred Structure fit everything, or having trouble sticking to it in the beginning.

As I said before, troubleshooting can be even more valuable than the original Bull's Eye exercise, because implementing Sacred Structure is going to act as a kind of a black light for what's NOT working for you. **I guarantee that if something is keeping you from using your time to the best of your ability, it's blocking you in other areas as well.**

It's important that we go into the troubleshooting aspect of making Sacred Structure work for you. This is where you're going to learn what's stood in your way so far – what's blocked you from bending time to your will and feeling in control of how you spend your time. AND, this might be where you realize that in order to master this for yourself, in order to really apply it effectively, you're going to want accountability, structure, and support. And that's NOT ONLY OK – it's to be expected.

Here are some common issues that my clients run up against:

- ★ I can't seem to stick to my Sacred Structure
- ★ Other things "get in the way"
- ★ Tasks take longer than I expected
- ★ I'm having trouble saying "no" to additional things that pop up that I feel obligated to spend time on

One of the most powerful growth edges that Sacred Structures will highlight for you is that of creating and defending healthy boundaries.

Often, prioritizing your time and getting clear about where you want your energy to go (and where you are NOT willing to have it go, anymore) is a magickally powerful moment of realizing where boundaries need to be set. The work then begins as you set and hold them.

We are SO used to being helpers, healers, nurturers, and leaders in our families, communities, and businesses.

For many women it's automatic to say "yes," and then figure out later how to incorporate yet *another* responsibility or task.

> *Sacred Structure will allow you to focus on what's most important so you can whittle your time and energy down to YOUR priorities.*

> *Make no mistake: the universe, needy friends and family, and your own unconscious will test you once you set up healthy boundaries. But you can do it. Because NOTHING will change your life more (because your time IS your life).*

If you find yourself running over set periods of time blocks, over-extending yourself, saying "yes" when you mean "maybe" or "no," and feeling requests pushed on you when you try and focus on the points in your Sacred Structure, then you're getting a healthy invitation to firm up and defend your boundaries.

This will be a turning point for you. It's HARD to set and hold healthy boundaries. You're going to have to examine your fears around letting people down, being judged, not being a "team player," and maybe even being called selfish.

But your own highest priorities, visions, and needs are WORTHY of being self-centered – who ELSE would make YOUR heart-centered priorities their highest focus?

This is one of those places where you'll rarely see people calling men "selfish" for being ambitious. For claiming their time, saying no, putting their aspirations and goals first. It's a cultural given for men, whereas we have all sorts of baggage around the same actions.

This is an example of how the work of becoming sovereign around your time and cultivating your definition of success is going to be different for women than it typically is for men.

I have a very personal attachment to boundaries: I have an immune disorder that I've been diagnosed with my entire adult life.

This means that I think of my energy as "spoons," a term coined by Christine Miserandino, who uses a spoon as a metaphoric unit of energy for people with immune disorders. People who count their "spoons" start the day with a certain number of "spoons" (a set amount of energy).

Each conversation, activity, or hardship (not enough healthy food, sleep, or the presence of stress) "costs" us a spoon. If we run out of spoons we run out of energy and can't "do" the rest of our day.

Since I was 19 years old (when I first got sick), I understood that my energy and focus is finite, and I'm wise with how I spend it. I know the activities and demands that cost more spoons than others, and I'm very careful and protective of my time and energy because I understand that it's finite.

Additionally, I'm a helper and a healer. I want to be in service to people. In my younger years that made me a much worse people-pleaser than I am today. Today I do my best, but I'm always putting myself and my needs first.

There are small, reasonable exceptions, but I always test them to make sure I'm not putting my health at risk.

For example, yesterday I spent all morning filling the back of my truck with over 1000 pounds of dog and cat food, driving an hour to distribute pet food to people in need, meeting with several members of my team (social interactions cost "spoons," usually, so I have to consider them), driving home while picking up a holiday tree on the way (more human interaction, physical exertion getting it into the truck, and a little stress driving home as I couldn't close the tailgate and worried all the way home about it falling out).

When I got home the Kid and her BFF badly wanted to go to Target to get some last-minute gifts, and I had two more pet pantry-related stops.

Did I WANT to go to Target? Not really. Would I rather skip it and get into bed with a book? Sure. Did I have the spoons to go? Yeah, I could do it.

So it's not that I don't do things I don't really want to, ever, especially for my family. But in the back of my mind I'm always considering if I need to stop moving, rest, or lay low, and I WILL say NO if that's the case.

I'm also an empath which means that I feel and absorb other people's feelings, moods, and energy deeply. If you and I spend time together and you're having a terrible day, I'll feel that energy. If I'm not careful I'll actually absorb it. When my hubby or the Kid is in a terrible mood it's very difficult for me to not feel it, too.

All of these are reasons that I've had to learn to protect myself and create tools and systems for making sure that I'm only, to the best of my ability, carrying my own energy and feelings – not yours, too. :-)

I've also had to learn to be aware of my tendency to want to help people and make them happy, something that used to make it very hard for me to feel sovereign over my time, because many other people's needs and requests could usurp my own plans or priorities.

Does any of this resonate for you?

When I work with women in my programs I give them a tool called the Boundary Checkpoint – if you'd like a free copy of that, say it with me... I put it on your page of bonus goodies! https://InArmsCoaching.com/bookfreegift

TRUE STORY: *Many women who struggle with Sacred Structure and bending time are simply struggling with creating and maintaining healthy boundaries.*

This work will NOT just impact your time. You'll find it influencing your finances. The rates you charge. The hours you work. The type of work and clients you accept. The amount of housework you do. Even your closest relationships.

So, if the above resonates for you, you need to get serious at this point and be honest with yourself about what you're willing to do to own your time. Make sure you also acknowledge what you are saying 'no' to if you are not currently willing to do this work.

It's important. It's your life.

Is there enough at risk to begin to work on setting and maintaining healthy boundaries that allow you to feel sovereign over your time?

Do you deserve that? Are your goals worthy of it? Is the work you're putting out into the world worth it – your service, message, magick?

If that's a yes, take that ideal schedule you wrote out for yourself and make sure it's somewhere where you can see it every day – think: your fridge, bathroom mirror, desk, etc.

Hell, tape it to a string and then hang it from the top of doorways you walk through all day. Let it actually hit you in the face. :-)

Here's a tool to get ahead of the challenge: Right now, make a list of any areas or relationships where you KNOW, right off, you're going to have to set boundaries.

This might look like: at your kid's school. At your paycheck job. With your parents or another family member who pushes your boundaries. With a volunteer position. With a spouse. Maybe even with yourself. With screens. With ending the work day at a desired time.

I'll need to set boundaries HERE:

★ _____

★ _____

★ _____

★ _____

★ _____

★ _____

Your achievements in this area are going to depend on you standing up for your time and your heart-centered priorities.

For instance, you might have old beliefs around prioritizing what's important to you instead of putting your family or other people's needs first.

★ There might be beliefs around your right to say "no" when someone else creates drama or hardship in their life.

★ There might be beliefs around "who am I?" to protect your time or say no to expectations or requests.

★ There might be beliefs around people needing you, or the skills and brilliance that you have, especially if it helps people to transcend their own struggles and challenges.

If you're an empath, you might be feeling people's distress to the extent that helping them to alleviate it DOES make you feel better but at the cost of your own work, visions, and self-care.

<u>Boundaries are absolutely essential to your strength, vision, and ability to make magick.</u>

They require focus and self-love. They require the belief that you are worth considering, that your time is precious, and that you get to control it no matter what other people want of you.

This is part of becoming sovereign – being in ownership of your time, energy, finances, and focus.

And yet, every woman I've ever worked with has work to do around setting and maintaining healthy boundaries.

So, the starting point for you, here, is to recognize if this is what's stopping Sacred Structure and the ability to bend time to your will in working for you and see if you can start to understand what these beliefs are.

Chapter 6

Connecting the Dots

Quick break here: I want to make sure that you SEE the connection between the work we're doing and the art and science of magick, because that's what the title of this book spoke to in you. It's part of why you grabbed it, I'm assuming.

Magick and alchemy are about taking what's happening (or is) and changing it into something ELSE that's happening (or is).

Alchemy historically was used for desires such as turning lead into gold (the most classic example).

Magick typically deals with turning loneliness into passionate partnership. Poverty into wealth. Illness into health. One stuck job into an exciting career.

For most of us who practice magick, the point is to manifest something that we want, or rid ourselves of something that we DON'T want.

From my teens until about two years ago, my magickal practices were delightfully witchy and full of pretty candles, crystals, and altars.

My magickal practices felt good to me. I loved connecting with the elements, nature, and myself. I loved the act of turning within to find answers and guidance. I loved ritual, making space to get present and focused, and all the tools of magick as most of us know them.

But it wasn't actually creating real change in my life or in my business.

It felt good. It was soothing, and allowed me to tap into a sense of empowerment over my thoughts, beliefs, and actions. Through my magickal practices I learned to move from reacting from my emotions to **responding** – choosing my response from my inner wisdom and intuition.

It was very late in my life that I started learning the deeper workings of magick – the magick-with-a-K that would actually start CHANGING the results I was seeing in both my personal and business life.

In order to be successful at magick and alchemy, one of the core pieces is that you have to learn to exert change within yourself before you can change anything: a result or situation OUTSIDE yourself.

In other words, you can burn candles and wear crystals until the cows come home, but **if you're not looking at your own fears, beliefs, and patterns of thinking** then nothing you do externally is going to fundamentally change the result you're seeing because that has to start with YOU.

If you want to change the fact that you attract partners who don't give you what you want, for example, who don't show up for you reliably, who don't make you happy, you have to START with what you believe is unlovable about you.

You have to start with why some part of you believes that you don't deserve the kind of love you dream of. You have to look at what you LOVE or are identifying with about being in unsatisfying relationships. Are you the one 'who never finds real love' in your mind? Has that become your identity?

Until you do THAT work, you can buy all the rose quartz and red candles that you want, and NO love spell, affirmations, or prayers are going to change the results you're seeing.

IF you want to attract a BOOMING business doing work you LOVE, work that feeds your soul and brings you abundant financial windfalls, then you first have to look at your beliefs around earning a thriving income from your skills and asking for what your time is worth. You have to look at your comfort with creating the visibility that allows the people who are looking for you to FIND you. You have to look at where you shy away from claiming your brilliance and the value of your work.

You have to look at where it's more comfortable to NOT look at the places you're not fully stepping into OWNERSHIP.

Until you do THAT, no green candles, crystals of prosperity, or external marketing strategies are going to change the results you're seeing.

You can't change what's happening outside until you change the programming inside. This is a fundamental premise of magick.

So, being able to change the results you're getting (aka magick) is about mastering what's happening in your head and heart first. (Which is what we've just begun working on together.)

Once you understand the base work of identifying what your stories are and making your unconscious, conscious, you can begin to work with what Carolyn Elliot calls "unified will," which basically means that **as you hit the gas pedal, all parts of you are moving cooperatively in the same direction. All parts of you are working in unity towards what you say you want.**

→ When you say you want more clients, no part of you is putting on the brakes out of fear of what that success might cost you.

→ When you say you want more free time, no part of you is pulling on the reins due to your fear of under-protected boundaries.

→ When you say you want LOVE, no part of you is putting on the kibosh because of that asshole you wound up with last time.

This allows you to move towards manifesting the results you want, like managing your time and creating way more of it wherein you're using it in a way that brings you joy.

The more you can master your own movement towards your joy, the more you can eliminate the blocks that have, up until now, stood in your way, the more magickal it will feel to focus on something and then be able to MAKE IT HAPPEN without sabotage.

This is the work I've done to start and grow a business while working full-time, AND while putting myself, my Kid, and my sanity FIRST. It only took me two years to bring in enough income to quit all other work.

This is the work I did to get my work week down to a general THREE days, while continuing to grow my business, so I could then start a non-profit dog rescue.

This is the work that's allowed me to keep growing BOTH, while spending 99.9% of my time doing EXACTLY what I want, what makes me most happy in any given moment, and **having more control and ownership over my time than almost anyone I know**.

...AND while adding a third business.

This is how I create time to rest, to arrange my schedule however it best serves me, to keep scaling and growing while keeping – and in some cases INCREASING – abundant amounts of free time.

The way I spend my time, the amount of free time I have, and the way I help my clients use this tool for their purposes FEELS incredibly magickal to me. It's about getting out of my own way, claiming ownership, and manifesting the results I desire OUTSIDE myself by doing work INSIDE myself and helping my clients do the same.

THE CULT OF BUSY

Let's circle back around now to what to look for when Sacred Structure doesn't work.

If you've already started implementing it, you're probably at the spot where the juicy stuff comes to the surface and you get to see your REAL blocks to time management that works for you.

If you're not, just come back to this section over and over again when you are, but it's good to read about it ahead of time so you have an idea of what might pop up as you start to implement it.

In the last chapter we explored how implementing Sacred Structure can bring boundary issues to the forefront, and some of the juicy and rewarding work you can do in that area.

{Side note: **if this were college this would be a 101 level class** – I just want to remind you of that. This book is an intro, a new way to begin to think about your time. It's a way to begin to explore your divided will, and to use magick in your personal and professional development. To really master time it's going to take more than one self-led book, so I want to prepare you for that.

I have clients who have been working with me for years and learn something new about magick and time management EVERY time we work on it. It's progress, not perfection, and I want to WELCOME you to a community in which you can continue this work and develop a sense of mastery eventually, if you're really enjoying the work.}

If boundaries feel like something that you're working through and pretty aware of, and yet time STILL doesn't feel like it's working for you, you might have either unconsciously drunk the Kool-Aid of the Cult of Busy, OR need actual personal support...or a combination of both.

Are any of these happening for you?

- ✴ I make blank time, and then I fill it instead of leaving time to rest/have unscheduled time, etc.

- ✴ I seem to jam-pack my schedule every week. Why can't I leave grace periods between blocks of time? I'm ALWAYS frantic.

- ✴ Even when I clear time I have an overwhelming urge to fill it – sometimes I don't even realize the urge and it just feels like the time "fills itself."

Oh, Boo. This issue is SO pervasive in our culture. Please recognize that you're not alone if this is part of what's happening for you.

If you take the "Cult of Busy" apart you'll find a complex root system that ultimately keeps us rushing, stuck in overwhelm, pitted against each other in competition, and discourages the connection with the self and access to our intuition and inner voice.

The Cult of Busy works on a similar premise as "no pain, no gain."

This highly addictive mentality hails from the patriarchal model of building a business: the hustle, the 80-hour-a-week mindset, the "identifying solely as what your work is," the "sacrifice-and-sweat = success" model.

Again, we see a framework by men, for men.

And again, it's built on the foundation of having a WIFE who handles and nurtures all the other areas of life so the man can focus on WORK. Career. Success.

It's a pillar of toxic masculinity that doesn't serve ANYONE: not the men who wind up feeling empty and disconnected, not the hetero women who lack present, joyful, connected partners, not the kids who grow up only seeing Dad at dinner or bedtime.

{This is really important: Criticizing toxic patriarchy isn't about bashing MEN. Men lose just as much from it as we do.}

The toxic patriarchal model doesn't work for ANYONE, but it sure as shit works for capitalism, the corporations, the financial world.

And promoting a culture of HUSTLE is one of the ways they keep folks running and working so hard that most of us don't ever get the time or support to QUESTION whether this is even what we want.

It feeds the capitalist machine of consumerism that began with the industrial revolution, when we found tools for mass production and needed to create demand for more and more shit so we could keep the factories producing and the people buying.

This could bring me to a whole other tangent, but I'm going to redirect us and point out that, as women, none of us live in 1950s nuclear families where WE have a wife who stays home to orchestrate our lives so we can be gone at the office 10 hours a day.

I don't think ANYONE reading this book would WANT that, even if we could have it. It's funny to even think about. The women like you that I work with want to do work you love, but you also want free time. Time for family, self, friends, passion projects, etc.

What also deeply influences us is the EVOLUTION of the Cult of Busy.

I can remember talking with my mama friends in the West Village in NYC when my Kid was little, comparing notes about how BUSY we were.

I was juggling a night job, building my biz during the day, while I was taking care of my 3-year-old, managing her social dates, 6 hours a week of nursery school, various appointments, and my own life and running our little household of 2.

I feel like I didn't BREATHE back then.

{Side note: Sully and I were cleaning out our closet the other weekend. In a box I found a small, dog-tag style necklace that had the word "breathe" stamped on it. When I first told my besties in NYC that I wanted – NEEDED – to move to Maine, they were really upset. "WHY? Why would you move from NYC???" And the best way I could say it was that in Maine, I felt like I could breathe. For my birthday that year one of my besties got me that necklace, "So you remember to breathe HERE, where your friends are." As much as I loved them I moved to Maine a few years later, and have always been able to breathe since. :-)}

The Cult of Busy carries a twisted badge of honor, of beliefs, that can look like any of the following:

"I'm KILLING myself, so we can all agree that I deserve whatever success I create."

"I'm working as hard as you. I'm not getting anything easily. I'm just like you." (Also, "I'm proving that I deserve this.")

"I'm SO busy that it's easy to see that I'm needed/important/depended on/valued by others."

Check it out for yourself: write out at least 15 reasons how you "win" or "benefit" from staying frantic and scattered, or from getting stuck in the "Cult of Busy."

For instance, here are some of the things I used to LOVE about being so busy and stuck in chaos that I had no time to think.

1. It gave me adrenaline and kept me in motion so I could keep moving, even though what I needed was rest.

2. It helped me to feel worthy of what I was creating – no one could say that I hadn't "earned" it.

3. I had a belief that to be worthy of success I have to look like I'm killing myself/driving myself crazy/ really working for it/struggling.

4. It upheld a toxic pattern I had with my mother. Sometimes during my childhood I felt like I had to "break" to get her attention and nurturing, so if I looked ragged and on the verge of breakdown I

hoped it would encourage people to help me. It also was the way I felt worthy of help and support.

5. It made me feel needed, important, wanted. "Having" people to respond to, help, lots of things to do, and places to be made me feel validated.

6. I was so used to using the energy I got from being frantic. As someone with an immune disorder, I realized that I became addicted to using adrenaline for energy because I was usually exhausted and run down and didn't know if I could provide it on my own. I had a fear that if I stopped running, or slowed down, I would just break and not be able to get moving again. I mean, it IS a basic rule of physics, right? An object in motion stays in motion. Are YOU that object?

Do any of these resonate for you? **What are some of YOUR attachments to being frantic, having "no" time, feeling stuck in chaos?**

The Adrenaline Rush As Fuel

I want to spend a minute talking about the dependency we develop on using the adrenaline rush that we get from staying in motion **as fuel.**

Our frantic pace of life causes stress, adrenal depletion, and massive wear and tear on our nervous systems to sustain. We rely more and more on external forms of energy (like sugar and caffeine) and the energy rush that we get from feeling frantic, rushing, panicked, frazzled.

This pace of life becomes addictive to the brain and body. It gets harder and harder to slow down, to focus on just ONE thing instead of many, and to turn inwards and listen to ourselves.

There are many repercussions of living this way, and one of the most dangerous (other than the obvious ramifications to your health from the stress) is the disconnect from self that happens when you are stuck in rushing all the time and the Cult of Busy.

When you're running on autopilot it becomes nearly impossible to connect inwards. To access your intuition and develop your ability to manifest, to make magick, to change energy, to evolve personally. It becomes difficult to make time to process where you are, what's working and what's NOT working, so that you can become more conscious about what your energy is pointed towards.

THIS affects your sacred work, your ability to have an impact, your peace of mind, and your access to being present and grounded.

Being separated from your ability to drop into your intuition, your inner voice, or gut KNOWING, has dangerous repercussions in your daily life as well as your business.

When you're not connected to the part of you that KNOWS, you're way more likely to flit around to various external sources of information or advice, investing in what others say is best, even if they don't even KNOW you or your work.

Many clients who come to me are self-described knowledge junkies. This can look like running from source of info to source of info, paying for e-courses, programs, books, or webinars...none of which REALLY changes the results you're getting...in a misguided belief that ALL the answers are "out there" and you can't access or trust your own voice and wisdom to steer you.

I'm not saying that you'll never need support, knowledge, or education, but if you're choosing investments without a connection to your own intuitive sense of what you need, then you have no filter, no compass, no guiding light that helps you decide, in a SEA of options, what's going to be most likely to work for YOU.

Additional Walls

Another wall you could be hitting if Sacred Structure isn't working for you is a small constellation of beliefs that look like one or all of the following:

* ★ I should be able to do everything by myself (this relates to delegation and stepping into leadership, which COULD be a book in and of itself)

* ★ I'm not worthy (of support, success, ease, financial stability and abundance)

* ★ And the myth of arrival belief, which misleads you into thinking that there's some magical point of "success" at which you finally "deserve" or can justify support...and you're not there yet

Do any of those resonate for you? It's not like winning a prize at the carnival – you get to pick **more than one** stuck belief or fear. Heck, sometimes you run through a range of them! I've had MANY of the ones that we've discussed so far, in different situations and at different times.

Cultivating the art and science of bending time is a journey, a path, a practice. I hope that in this book you've begun to understand some of the most important parts: namely, why you block yourself from being able to create sovereignty over your time in the first place.

I also hope that you don't stop here. This has simply been the beginning of changing the way you think about time, boundaries, and your own journey and evolution.

I hope this has whetted your appetite for diving deeper into getting support around cultivating sovereignty: over your time, your energy, and your finances.

So you can begin to build the life you *actually* want to live.

At this point, you should have a clear idea of what is working for you around your time, and how to make more of it.

I imagine you've learned some juicy and valuable pieces around how you benefit (or some part of you believes that you benefit) from NOT having time work for you.

You can see the connection between being able to get out of your own way, to seeing your visions clearly and manifesting them, and more powerfully: what KEEPS you from having the things you say you want, or that you're working for.

My hope is that you'll use the content of this book to spark your journey towards building a life that's YOURS.

Where you're sovereign over your time and energy, and spending it on what you love.

Where you're working in your zone of genius, with all your energy and focus at your disposal.

Where you're using the tools you've learned here to flush out any areas where your will is divided and you're wasting energy trying to move forward with your brakes on.

Now you can take what we've done over the course of our time together and begin to build on it.

And if you know you could use some extra help, clarity, support or community, I invite you to reach out to me. I'd love to hear from you – just shoot me an email at britt@ inarmscoaching.com.

If you know you're ready to make moves to grow your business while creating the schedule of your dreams, check out my available programs. Each one a game-changer in its own right and the exercises in this book are taken from a course that I'll tell you about when you grab the bonus gift offer, which comes with a bunch of additional work that we didn't have room for in this book.

The course I'll tell you about also has one of the most IMPORTANT factors that leads to success for my clients: *personalized, in-real-time, direct support of YOU, by ME. It's not just spoon-fed content that you have to adapt, all by yourself, to your growth.*

Additionally, it's got support from a community of other like-minded women who get you, cheer you on, and value your presence as you all move through the course together.

I'd love to work with you directly and hold your hand while you create an impact, an income, and INFLUENCE with your work. Just grab the bonus gift kit that I've offered throughout the book, and I'll send you more information about working with me personally to implement these tools- and SO MUCH MORE. Come check it out: https:// InArmsCoaching.com/bookfreegift

Because we need you.

We need your magick.

We need your strength.

We need your passion, your presence, and your special talents and wisdom.

We need you at the table.

I trust this book has given you first steps to make the SPACE to ignite the passion that there's room for when you change the way you spend your time. I hope you join us to change the world, one small corner at a time.

All hands on deck, magnificent. I'll see you there.

Epilogue

 A Special Bonus from Britt

Now that you've read **The Magick of Bending Time in Your Sacred Business,** you're on your way to understanding how to avoid struggling with too much on your plate as you build your business.

I'm deeply committed to combating the common feelings that women like you and I have that you're always too busy and don't have enough time for everything you want. I think you understand (or will, when you finish this book) how this can be a true SUCCESS KILLER.

I'm excited that you can understand WHY time management hasn't worked for you up until now, and the inner pieces that must be examined before you can make time work for you in a sustainable way.

I'd love to give you a special bonus I created to add to the work in this book: **The Bending Time Gift Kit,** which is a way to take a few next, powerful steps to make this content work in a more hands-on way after finishing the book (or alongside your reading!).

There's so much confusing information out there about time management for women with sacred work and multi-passionate entrepreneurs – much of it written by people who DON'T understand your unique problems around managing and structuring your time.

As you finish this book you'll be armed with what you need to know to set and maintain healthy boundaries around your time...AND a few powerful next steps to continue to build on the work (possibly even directly with me and my live support).

While the tools in the **Bending Time Gift Kit** are often offered for sale, as a bonus for buying this book you can claim it for free here:

https://InArmsCoaching.com/bookfreegift

As another bonus, when you sign up for the toolkit I'm going to take you to where **magick meets business** and share some of my **FAVORITE result-changing tools** with you. You may, of course, opt out at any time.

The sooner you know how to bend time, the better your chances for building the wealth, impact, and influence that you dream of having with your work – WITHOUT the fear of what it might COST you.

I'm in your corner. Let me know how I can help further.

Here's to magickal time bending, and your success!

Best,

Britt

Acknowledgments

I grew up reading typewritten pages of my mother's manuscripts.

My first, and deepest gratitude goes to my mother, published author, Jamie Pastor Bolnick. You would do yourself a favor to go find both her books and read them. She taught me to love reading and to connect with people through stories that I could communicate through my writing.

I have LONG wanted to publish my own book and my mother is one of the greatest parts of that desire. I am also eternally grateful for her proofreading of this manuscript and the kind-yet-firm removal of probably no less than a few hundred commas.

Second deepest gratitude goes to my soulmate, the Kid, Bella Nysa Pastor. Her birth put me on a path that has been so rich, so beautiful, so sacred, so full of joy (and snot, and tears, and painful growth).

She is hands down the FUNNIEST person I know, one of the absolutely wisest, and probably the most beautiful soul I will ever meet. This book is being published as she flexes her wings in preparation to leave the nest. While I will miss her like I'd miss both my arms if they were severed from my body, the work that I've done in being the best mama possible to her has filled my life with so MANY things that I love that I know I'll survive her flight away. (Or, I'm optimistic that I'll survive it. I'd be lying if I said I was 100% sure.)

I am so grateful to my husband and step-daughter, Sully and Riley Rose, because they have partnered with us to build a most wonderful life. Sully is the anchor to my ambitious visions, the practical foundation-builder to our dreams, and catches all the bugs in the house (except the spiders, whom I love). He is the mouse-trap emptier, the trailer-to-the-truck hitcher, the one who makes broken things work again. The joyful, passion-filled work I get to spend my time on would not be possible without his counterweight.

And Riley Rose – well, suffice to say that she's the Kid I wished for but didn't get to give birth to, if that makes any sense. I know that if Bella and I could CHOOSE a sister for her, Riley would have been it, so super cool that it just worked out that way. These two goofs fill the house with laughter, silliness, so much art and creativity, and I can't WAIT to see what THEY create in the world with their precious time.

I am grateful to my best boo, Jennifer Moore, of Modern Medicine Lady.com, who has been a support beam to me since...well, forever I think. She is one of the main reasons Bella and I moved to Maine, which is where all the happiness began. She is there when I'm sad, when I'm scared, when I'm sick. She's just there. I was immensely inspired by HER release of HER book, "*Empathic Mastery*," a year before mine, (and yes, you NEED TO READ IT, so go look it up) and her book-birthing inspired and motivated me to get my shit together and get this book out into the world.

I am also grateful for the support of Nikki Starcat Shields, a long-time client and book midwife, who edited this book and helped the process of birthing it into the world, and my book launch coach, Diana M. Needham, as well as Katie Owen, who helped mold the content to serve you in the most effective way possible – without the three of them this book would have been massively difficult to achieve joyfully.

Christi Cooper is my beloved branding and tech support goddess, and she's responsible for taking my heart and soul and making pictures that represent them – she's done many of the beautiful graphics (and the cover designs!) that you see.

I am SO grateful for all the women whom you see endorsements from. These are some of the women in my life that I am deeply grateful to and whose support I cherish.

Jen Spivak lit the fire under my ass that became this book. In telling me about an ad campaign she was running for a client, she said that their most successful ad copy said that the woman "LITERALLY wrote the book on _____." And that got me thinking: what could I say I "literally wrote the book" on? And now you're holding it. Isn't that cool?

I am beyond grateful for my teams – the literal arms that support me: both the Pittie Posse team and my In Arms Coaching team. They are full of some of the most incredible women (and a few good men) that I have EVER met.

When I say I couldn't have built this life without them I'm not speaking metaphorically – I really couldn't have. They compensate for my weakness. They take as much as possible off my plate so I can envision bigger and bigger. They surround me when the trolls attack. They help me build. They SEE my dreams, get equally excited, and roll up their sleeves with me. Teamwork DOES make the dream work.

To my teachers/mentors/coaches, namely Joanna Lindenbaum, you have shown me how to combine healthy boundaries with magical leadership. Thank you.

The path to joy and fulfillment is not meant to be walked alone. In fact, if you BELIEVE you have to walk it alone it's incredibly difficult to achieve. At each step of the way I have been held by the support, wisdom, mentorship, and teachings of other women, and Joanna is one who has literally changed my life. I would not be where I am today without her wisdom and brave role-modeling.

I would be remiss in not mentioning here my gratitude for Jupiter.

Ahhh, Jupiter.

Carolyn Elliot taught me how to work with planetary magic in her mind-blowing course, INFLUENCE, and I'd say that Jupiter and I are still in dating-mode.

We haven't done the deed yet, but I keep plugging along, side-stepping my resistance and self-sabotage, to woo Jupiter into a hot-and-heavy relationship.

That being said, I am grateful for the inspiration and gravitational pull of the biggest planet in our system, with his swirly cloud stripes and his favorable disposition towards business success, expansion, prosperity and visibility. I will continue to court his influence and good favor.

And a huge nod of gratitude for punk rock, namely the Rudimentary Peni station on Pandora. This book was written with a soundtrack of bad-ass punk rock and industrial tunes, including but not limited to Hole, Conflict, Bad Brains, Distillers, Minor Threat, NitzerEbb, Brody Dalle, and Nausea.

About the Author

Britt is owner and founder of In Arms Coaching, the co-founder of Pittie Posse Rescue, and the creatrix of *Sacred Structure* and the *Bending Time tools*, which she has polished and perfected over 15 years of using them to raise a child as a solo-parent while building a thriving business, a bad-ass pit bull rescue, and caring for a marauding bunch of derpy pit bulls and humorless chickens at home.

She shares her home in the Maine woods with two incredible teen girls, a sexy-ass husband who fixes things, and the aforementioned troupe of demanding animals.

Some of her favorite things are her daughter's wicked sense of humor, cayenne in her coffee, fresh oysters from the Damariscotta River, really cold, clean sheets on the bed, walks in the woods, and floating down pretty much any river in Maine. She and her husband spend more and more of the warm months off grid in their travel trailer, kayaking, reading, and grilling too much delicious food.

Printed in Great Britain
by Amazon

20011471R00112